UNION ☆ BOUND

UNION★BOUND

WILLIAM R. WALTERS & MICHAEL DAVIS

UNION BOUND

Published by WND Books, Washington, D.C. WND Books is a registered trademark of WorldNetDaily.com, Inc. ("WND")

Book designed by Mark Karis

WND Books are available at special discounts for bulk purchases. For more information call (541) 474-1776, e-mail orders@wndbooks.com, or visit www.wndbooks.com.

Paperback ISBN: 978-1-944229-25-2
eBook ISBN: 978-1-944229-26-9

Library of Congress Cataloging-In-Publication Data

Printed in the United States of America
16 17 18 19 20 21 PAH 9 8 7 6 5 4 3 2 1

It is well that war is so terrible—lest we grow fond of it.
—GENERAL ROBERT E. LEE, BATTLE OF FREDERICKSBURG, 1862

CONTENTS

One day my office phone rang, and a sweet voice came through the line. "Hi, this is Pam Jay, and I own the consignment shop up the street. I was wondering could you meet my husband, Bill, and I for coffee. We want to talk to you about a project that involved one of my ancestors?"

When you work in the film industry everyone seems to have an idea—a one sheet or a script—but a thought flashed through my mind: "What if this is a great story? How amazing would that be?" I agreed to meet them and thought, "what's the worst that can happen? I have coffee with two nice people."

A few days later I went to the coffee shop around the corner where I met Pam and Bill. After chit chatting a bit, Pam put a plastic box and three-ring binder on the table. She slowly took the lid off the box. With a twinkle in her eye she looked at me and says, "These are the surviving diaries of my great-great grandfather which have been passed down in our family." She slowly pulled out a cloth in which two very small books were wrapped. On one was written the date 1863 and on the other 1864. She continued, " He fought in the Civil War and survived. He even won some medals."

I am not a historian, but I love history. I have a deep interest in the Civil War, and so to hear about a man who survived the carnage of the worst war in the history of the United States definitely got my attention.

She began to tell me about Sgt. Joseph Hoover of the 121st New York Volunteers while pulling out more and more things from this treasure box. She showed me Sergeant Hoover's medals, pictures, and pins. She opened the three-ring binder. "These are his war records. These are his medical records, and this is his discharge paper from the army." On and on the story kept getting better.

Bill who had been patiently sitting sipping his coffee and listening chimed in and explained that Pam Jay is the great-great granddaughter of Joseph Hoover. Pam's father, Robert Forster, gave Bill the diaries in the 1990s. He began transcribing them. The entries were in pencil and not easy to read, and the various terms of the period used by Joseph were often difficult to understand. Bill also researched Hoover's military and medical records and the history of his unit. The records corroborated Joseph Hoover's diary entries. Other family members wanted to help, so Pam's cousins Pat and Bryan Ennis helped with additional transcribing and research.

Bill went on to explain as he handed me a printout, "this is the transcript of the 1864 diary that Pat, Bryan, and I painstakingly transcribed page by page. What's interesting is he was captured at the Battle of the Wilderness and was sent to Andersonville prison for four months. Then he was sent to Florence, South Carolina, to a new camp that was still being built. After about four days he and a friend escaped the prison camp and ended up being saved by slaves and made it all the way to New Bern."

As Bill was talking I was seeing a movie in my mind—a

daring prison escape, gunfire, dogs, guys being chased in the woods. "This is amazing," I said. "What do you want to do with this material?" Without hesitating Pam said, "We want to honor him by telling his story in a documentary."

"What if we turned it into a feature film?" I asked.

"Do you think it is possible?"

"From all that you have told me and what I have seen here I think this story needs to be on the big screen."

The wheels began turning. A friend of mine, John Errington, who has a degree in historical studies from Harvard, agreed to write the screenplay. With a powerful script, we were able to attract the necessary actors and funds, and as they say, the rest is history.

The fact that Joseph took the time during that brutal war to tell his own story is truly remarkable. He has given us the opportunity to show the world what a bold, clever, resourceful, and good person he truly was.

This experience is such an honor and privilege, not given to many. I hope that in reading his story, you will walk away with a deeper concern for American history and for the people that came before us. We are all Americans, no matter our race, our color, or our background, and this story shows that we can overcome our struggles when we join together in purpose.

I want to thank everyone involved in making the movie *Union Bound* and to William R. Walters for writing this book with me. It's been such a huge effort on the part of so many talented people, and an especially rewarding experience for Bill and Pam Jay, Pat and Bryan Ennis, and all of Joseph Hoover's descendants who are so proud of their great-great grandfather Joseph Hoover of the 121st.

Hoover's amazing experiences have inspired us all.
I hope you are inspired too.

—MICHAEL DAVIS

UNION★BOUND

THURSDAY, JULY 24, 1862

ENLISTMENT DAY, LITTLE FALLS, NY

Joseph Hoover stood next to his horse and stared at the Little Falls Mercantile. He wiped beads of sweat from his brow and squinted at the sun. It was still early in the morning, and the sun was barely above the treetops, but the heat had already started. It would be another hot day. Joseph removed his worn overcoat and slung it over his saddle.

A crowd had begun to form around the veranda of the mercantile, their attention fixed on a one-armed Union soldier standing next to a small table. The soldier's uniform was clean, the brass buttons of his frock coat glinting in the morning sun. Despite missing an arm, the man appeared impressive, his bushy mustache curled neatly at the ends. The slightly rakish slant of his kepi gave him the air of an experienced officer.

Joseph noticed the officer's sword still hung from his belt on the left side despite his not having a right arm. He wondered how the man would be able to draw his sword, then realized the officer no longer had a reason to. A pang of sympathy flushed his cheeks and he looked away.

A cloud of dust kicked up by the gathering crowd moved slowly down the street, and Joseph pushed his horse back as he stepped out of its path. He had taken a bath the night before and had no intentions of presenting himself with dirt clinging to his sweaty face.

Joseph watched as another soldier, a sergeant, stepped out from the mercantile and began placing sheets of paper and an inkpot on the table, making sure that the papers were squared and the inkpot placed just so.

The officer standing next to the table waited patiently, his hand rising now and then to stroke his mustache in an almost affectionate way.

Joseph's hand mirrored the soldier's actions, but his fingers found only the short hairs of his young mustache, and the notion of stroking it seemed useless. He let his hand drop and shifted his feet uncomfortably.

"Is everything ready, Sergeant?" the officer asked finally, looking around at the growing crowd.

"Yes, sir!" the sergeant answered sharply.

The officer nodded and took a step forward, his eyes traveling over the people. Joseph followed his gaze and saw that many of those gathered were young men. Some had come with family; others, alone, but all of them appeared nervous.

The officer cleared his throat in a loud and important way.

"Good morning," he said. "My name is Captain Burrows. You all know why I'm here today, so I'll dispense with the usual long-winded speech." He rested his left hand on the pommel of his saber. "I know some of you have come here with your families—mothers and fathers, brothers and sisters—and it warms my heart that you are here, supporting those who would come forward."

The officer adjusted his stance before continuing. "I would speak now to those who will soon come forward and put their names on the roster and swear their fealty to the Union."

There was a slight stirring in the crowd as young men separated themselves from their families and moved to the front. Joseph looked around and saw a hitching post next to the veranda. He pulled his horse up and tied the reins before stepping back. He looked to his left and found himself standing next to an older man dressed in worn clothes and a floppy, wide-brimmed hat. Joseph was surprised to see gray streaks in the man's otherwise black beard.

"Are you here in support of your son?" Joseph asked.

The gentleman turned, and Joseph was taken aback by the sadness he saw in the older man's eyes.

"I am here to volunteer," he said quietly.

"Surely your family needs you, sir."

The man stood silently, and Joseph wondered if he had overstepped his bounds. "I mean no offense, sir," he apologized.

"None taken," the stranger replied. "My son was killed during the Battle of Hoke's Run a year ago this month." He took off his hat and wiped his brow. "It broke my wife's heart. She died of fever of the lung this past Christmas."

"I am truly sorry for your loss," Joseph said. He lowered his head and stared at his shoes.

"I have made my peace with God." The man put his hat back on. "Do you think they will take me?"

The question hung in the air between them.

"I do not know, sir."

"I am old. I know this. But I am still strong and a good shot with my rifle."

Joseph bobbed his head. "Then I am sure they will." He stuck out his hand. "My name is Joseph. Joseph Hoover."

The man shook Joseph's hand warmly. "Jacob Gardner."

The officer on the veranda cleared his throat again, and the two men fell silent.

"This is the last day we will be in Little Falls." The officer surveyed the men standing before him. "I had hoped for a larger gathering of men." He sighed. "Perhaps more will come as the day moves on.

"All of you are here to answer your country's call," he went on. "We need good, strong young men to bring the Southern states back into the Union and end this war."

"When will it end?"

All heads turned to the families who stood behind the men. One of the mothers had stepped forward, ignoring her husband's attempts to keep her still. "When will it end?" she asked again. There was no mistaking how poor this mother and father were. Both were dressed in clothes that had been mended almost to the point that there was more stitching than cloth.

The officer shot the woman a glare. "Madam, I assure you that the war will be ended before Christmas. Even now our forces are harrying the enemy on several fronts. It is only a matter of time before they come to their senses and surrender."

"That is what we were told when our oldest boy signed that piece of paper," she said, pointing an accusing finger at the stack of papers on the table. "He was blown up not more than a month ago." Tears began rolling down her face, leaving trails in the dust that covered her cheeks. "We had *two* sons. Now you take our last, and he not more than a week past eighteen."

Everyone turned to look for the younger son. He was not hard to spot. He stood with his head down, his cheeks red either from anger or embarrassment, or perhaps both, Joseph thought.

The officer cleared his throat again. "Perhaps, sir," he said, addressing the boy's father, "if you could control your wife, we can begin."

The woman's husband wrapped his arms around his wife and whispered into her ear as he pulled her back. Joseph watched as the woman collapsed in tears, the husband finally forced to half carry, half drag her from the roadway.

"Now," the officer continued, "if you gentlemen would be so good as to form a line at the foot of these steps, we can finish this before the heat becomes overpowering."

Joseph moved with the other men and lined up. He and Jacob were the last in line, and it took almost an hour before Joseph reached the bottom of the steps.

The sun was now overhead, the heat and dust becoming stifling. Sweat ran freely down Joseph's face, and his white shirt was drenched and clinging to him. He shuffled his feet uncomfortably as he waited for the man ahead of him to finish signing his name.

"Next!" the sergeant bellowed.

Joseph climbed the short steps and stood before the table.

The sergeant shuffled some papers until he found one that

was blank. He dipped the pen in the ink pot, giving the pen one sharp shake to make sure the ink didn't drip.

"Name," he called out. "Family name first, Christian name second."

Joseph's voice seemed to leave him just then, and he barely heard himself when he answered, "Hoover, Joseph."

The sergeant leaned over the table. "You ashamed of your name, boy?" he growled.

"No, sir." Joseph shook his head. He heard some of the men standing in the street chuckling.

"Then why are you whispering it?" The sergeant squinted his eyes. "Say it loud and proud, son."

"Hoover, Joseph!"

"That's better." The sergeant scribbled Joseph's name onto the sheet. "But I'm not deaf."

"No, sir."

The sergeant took down Joseph's age before yelling, "Next!"

Joseph stepped away from the table and almost stumbled down the steps. He took his place in the crowd and waited.

The sergeant wrote down Jacob's name but paused when the older man said his age. "Captain," he called out.

Joseph edged slowly toward the steps to hear what was being said.

"This man says he's forty," the sergeant told the officer.

The captain stroked his mustache as he considered Jacob. "You're a bit older than most recruits."

Jacob just shrugged his shoulders.

"You understand, sir, that this is a volunteer company?"

"I do," Jacob answered.

"What about your family? Your wife, she is resigned to this?"

"My wife died six months ago," Jacob said. "Our only child was killed last year at Hoke's Run."

"My condolences, sir," the captain said, then asked, "Are you suffering any ailments? Your eyesight good?"

Joseph stepped forward and, before Jacob could answer, spoke up. "He's strong as a bull and an excellent shot with a rifle."

The sergeant sprang to his feet. "Was the captain talking to you"—he glanced down at Joseph's sheet—"Mr. Hoover?"

The captain waved his remaining hand, dismissing the sergeant. "It is quite all right, sergeant." He pointed at Joseph. "Are you standing in witness to this man's abilities?"

"I am, sir."

"Very well then. Sergeant, keep this man's name on the roll." He smiled at Jacob. "It may ease your concern to know that you are not the oldest man to volunteer here. Isn't that right, sergeant?"

The sergeant snapped a salute. "Yes, sir!" He shuffled the papers together and put the lid on the ink pot before standing at attention next to the officer.

The captain turned his attention to the men still gathered in the street. "Gentlemen, you have now enlisted in the Union Army for a term of three years. You will, in one hour, gather here and march to camp Schuyler outside of Herkimer to begin your training. Use this hour to say your farewells." The Captain stepped off the veranda and walked briskly up the street, the sergeant following close behind.

"Why did you lie for me?"

Joseph turned and found Jacob standing with his face only inches from his own. "Were you lying to me?" Joseph asked.

The question took Jacob by surprise. "No," he answered.

"Then I wasn't lying."

Jacob stared at Joseph for a moment. "Thank you," he said finally.

Joseph smiled and untied his horse.

"What will you do with your horse?"

Joseph leaned against the mare and patted its withers. "I hadn't thought about it. I should have left her back on the farm."

"Maybe the army will buy her," Jacob suggested.

Joseph smiled. "I think they will see her for what she is, old and tired." He stroked the horse's mane fondly. "There's a blacksmith up the street. I'll take her there and see what I can get for her and the saddle."

"Probably best."

Joseph tugged on the reins and led the horse up the street.

A half hour later he returned with his roll and coat slung over his shoulders. He looked at the coins in his hand.

"He took the horse?" Jacob was sitting on the steps of the mercantile, whittling on a piece of wood.

"Yup," Joseph replied. "Ten dollars for the horse and saddle. He tried to give me pieces of paper he called 'greenbacks.'"

Jacob frowned. "Huh," he grunted. "I heard of 'em." He spat on the ground. "Give me good ol' silver and gold coins any day."

"That's what I said." Joseph peered into the open door of the mercantile. "Think I'll go in and see what there is to see."

Jacob tossed the stick he had been working on and stood up. "Mind if I join you?"

"Not at all."

The two men entered the store and stood just inside the

threshold. It took a bit for their eyes to adjust, and when they did, all they could do was stare.

"Lord Almighty," Joseph breathed. Items of every description either hung from the ceiling and walls or were stacked on tables that ran the length of the store.

"I don't reckon I seen so much packed into one place ever," Jacob added.

Joseph moved into the store, his head turning this way and that as his eyes took in everything. He stopped in front of a table laden with clothes and picked up a pair of gray wool socks.

"I imagine the army will supply us with socks," Jacob said.

"Don't count on it," a voice from behind them growled.

Joseph and Jacob turned to see the owner of the store standing behind a counter. He was balding with a bushy gray mustache and beard. He stood with his arms folded across his chest and a hard look in his eyes.

"Why not?" Joseph asked.

"Think about it. Thousands of men, all needin' socks." The man spat on the floor behind the counter. "I'm guessing you'll both be barefoot in yer boots before the week's out."

"And it could be that you'll say anything to part a man from his money." Jacob eyed the man suspiciously.

"Don't make no never mind to me. Buy, don't buy, but if all you're gonna do is stand there gawkin', you can do it outside."

Joseph grabbed a pair of socks. "How much?"

"Five pennies a pair," the owner said.

Joseph looked at the socks in his hand and then grabbed two more pairs. He moved to another table. Joseph didn't touch anything, afraid his dirty hands would ruin the new articles.

He took a breath and smelled something familiar. As he

stepped back toward the counter, his face broke into a smile.

"How much?" he asked, tilting his head at the large wooden barrel filled with brine and floating pickles.

"Penny each."

"You hungry?" Joseph asked Jacob.

"Yes," Jacob answered. "But I ain't got no money."

Joseph reached a hand in and pulled out two big pickles. "I'm guessing we won't get a chance to eat until we get to camp." He saw some loose paper and wrapped the pickles before stepping up to the counter. Joseph placed the pickles and socks on the counter and turned to the store owner. "Where is the post office?"

"Y'er lookin' at it."

"I need a piece of paper and an envelope."

The owner put a piece of blank paper and a thick, brown envelope on the counter. "Penny a piece."

"You gonna charge us for the air?" Jacob asked.

"Would if I could." The owner glared back.

Joseph saw a pencil sticking from behind the owner's ear and grabbed it. "I'm just borrowing," he said and began writing on the paper. When he was done, he took nine of the silver dollars and slid them into the envelope.

The owner lit a candle and handed it across the counter to Joseph. Joseph tipped the candle and dripped wax onto the envelope to seal it.

"How long to get this to Utica?" he asked as he wrote, "Hoover Farm, Utica New York" on the envelope.

"Couple, three days."

Joseph nodded. His eye caught a leather-bound book, and he picked it up. The cover was wrapped with a soft leather string. He unraveled it and opened the book.

"What is this?" he asked, thumbing through the blank pages.

"That there is a diary," the owner answered. "For keeping track of your daily doin's."

Joseph smiled. "How much?"

"That's good leather and high-quality paper. Fifty cents."

"How much for everything?" Joseph asked.

The owner counted the items on the counter. "Including the postage, seventy cents in all."

Joseph laid his remaining dollar on the counter.

The owner counted out the change and handed it to Joseph.

"You might want to count it," Jacob advised, tossing the owner a glare of his own.

"Don't fret it," Joseph said. He stuffed the two pairs of socks into his roll.

"I want my pencil back," the owner complained.

Joseph flicked a penny at the man and left the store.

The two men sat down on the top step. Joseph handed Jacob one of the pickles and bit into his own. Brine ran freely down his chin, and his mouth puckered at the sharp flavor.

Jacob took a bite of his pickle and chewed thoughtfully. "This is a good pickle. My wife made good pickles."

"My mom does too." Joseph answered, then took another bite and stared out onto the street.

"You gonna put those socks on here?" Jacob asked.

Joseph looked at the pair of socks in his hand and smiled. He extended them out to Jacob.

The older man shook his head.

"Take 'em," Joseph insisted. "Maybe one day we're in some battle and you'll remember these socks and save my life."

Jacob laughed. "That might be the only way I can pay you

back." He took the socks and looked at them. "I thank you," he said quietly.

The two men sat in silence, eating their pickles. Soon, men began filling the street in front of the mercantile. Their families returned with them but hung back.

"What do you think it will be like?" Joseph asked.

Jacob shrugged. "Bad enough, I guess."

Joseph pushed himself to his feet and brushed the dust off his pants. "I guess it's time."

"Yes," Jacob said and stood. "It will be a long walk."

The captain returned riding a black mare, the sergeant jogging beside him. He reined in the horse but stayed in the saddle as he addressed the men assembled.

"Sergeant, form the men in ranks."

The sergeant snapped a salute. "Yes, sir!" He spun on his heels and bellowed, "When I call, 'Fall in,' everyone will form up in ranks of four abreast." The sergeant took a deep breath. "FALL IN!"

The men milled about, looking at each other.

The sergeant sighed and spat in the dirt. "When a sergeant such as myself calls, 'Fall in,' you will come forward and stand"—he pointed at the dirt in front of his feet—"here, here, here, and here. The next men will line up behind the first in rows of four."

The sergeant pushed his kepi forward and took another deep breath. "FALL IN!"

Joseph and Jacob looked at each other before moving to stand in front of the sergeant. The other men slowly formed ranks, the sergeant moving up and down the lines, yelling until he was satisfied that everyone was standing where they should be.

"Are the men ready, sergeant?" the captain asked.

The sergeant took off his cap and scratched his head. "I don't know about ready, sir, but they are all pointed in the same direction. What happens after that, only the good Lord knows."

"That will have to do, sergeant. Move them out." The captain spurred his horse into a walk.

"Company, MARCH!" the sergeant roared.

"I think you are right, Jacob. This *is* going to be a long walk." Joseph moved forward as the man behind him stepped on his heels.

MONDAY, AUGUST 11, 1862

TRAINING, CAMP SCHUYLER

Joseph wandered past tents and cooking fires as he made his way back to the large oak tree he and some of the other members of his platoon had been calling home for the last two weeks. He had been put in Company A of the 121st New York Infantry Regiment as soon as he and Jacob had arrived at the camp. Jacob's name was called for Company C, and since then Joseph had only caught the odd sighting of his new friend.

There had been little time to go look for him after the first day. From before sunrise to long after sunset, they trained. At first it was endless hours of marching and drilling until he thought his feet would fall off. The hobnailed boots the army had given him were stiff and unforgiving when he first put them on, but after a few days they had more or less broken in and the marching became easier, and by the end of the first week, even the pain in his lower back had left.

The second week had been filled with learning to load and fire the Enfield rifle they were each issued. The sergeant had the platoon drill with the rifles for two days before they were even issued ammunition. Joseph went over the counts in his mind as he walked. It took everyone over a minute to load the rifle once, not counting aiming and firing. The drill sergeant had walked along the line, yelling and cursing everyone. "You oughta be able to load and fire three times in a minute!" He'd yell.

By the end of the first day, Joseph could load and fire twice before the sergeant called time. By the end of the second day, he was working on four. The sergeant had clapped him on the back and told him he had the makings of a good soldier. Joseph was used to firing the old flintlock squirrel musket on the farm, but firing at your supper and firing on another human—who was firing back—was something different, and he wondered whether he would pull the trigger or freeze.

He adjusted the rifle slung over his shoulder and hefted the burlap sack he carried, a smile creeping onto his face. When he reached the tree, he saw that the other five soldiers had built up the fire and were huddled around it. Joseph could see the exhaustion in their upturned faces as they watched him approach their circle.

"We was beginning to think you'd deserted."

"Not before you, Robert." Joseph smiled at the young man and handed him the sack. "I think I got what we need." Joseph shrugged the rifle off his shoulder and leaned it against the tree before sitting down next to Robert. He had liked the young man almost as soon as he saw him grinning at the sergeant who was screaming into his face.

Robert opened the sack and his own smile faded. "Hardtack," he muttered.

"There's more than that." Joseph grabbed the sack and turned it over, spilling the contents onto the grass.

Everyone leaned forward to see rations of bacon and beef among the many wafers of hardtack.

"If we had a pot, we could make us a stew," Joseph commented.

Robert's grin returned. "Well, isn't that the trick?" He laughed. "Mort here managed to nick just such an item." He slapped the back of another man whose face looked younger than Robert's.

Joseph smiled and stretched out his legs before pulling the diary from inside his tunic. He unraveled the leather string and thumbed through the pages he had already written on. He stopped and looked around at the faces of his small group, trying to recall what it was that had brought them together.

Joseph glanced over at Ash Beckerman. At forty-one he was the oldest of the group. He complained little and spoke less, preferring to answer a question with a nod or a shake of his graying head.

Next to Ash sat the group's corporal and Mort's older brother, Henry Tinnerman. He was the mirror opposite of his younger brother. Mort carried the carefree air of youth with him and was quick to laugh. Henry was serious and hovered over his younger brother like a mother bear. He sat quietly rubbing his chin while Mort and Robert prepared the fixings for the stew.

"You stole the pot?" Henry asked quietly.

Joseph felt the whole group stiffen and the talking died down.

"Wouldn't call it stealin', really," Mort said.

"Did you pay fer it?" Henry shot back.

Even the crackling of the fire seemed to quiet down.

"It was a sutler," Mort answered sullenly. "You knows how they are. Bunch of vultures following the camps and chargin' extra for the stuff they knows we need."

"Don't matter." Henry kicked at a log half sticking out of the fire. "And you know it don't."

"You're not my pappy," Mort said, anger flushing his cheeks.

"No, I ain't. If Pappy was here, he'd beat you raw."

Mort had nothing to say about that and hung his head.

"It's not really stealin' if you're stealin' from a thief," Robert put in. "Is it, Joe?"

Everyone turned to look at Joseph.

Joseph glanced at Henry, who was looking at him hard, wondering which way he would go.

Joseph closed his diary and scratched the beard that had begun growing on his face. "How much was he askin' for the pot?"

"He wanted five greenbacks!" Mort almost shouted.

Even Ash made a noise at the cost.

"Don't matter if'n he was askin' fifty," Henry growled, his eyes still glued to Joseph.

"No," Joseph agreed. "It don't. My folks always taught me two wrongs don't make a right." He looked at Henry. "I was asking 'cause we're all gonna put in a greenback to pay for it." He turned to Mort. "Tomorrow you're gonna go back to the sutler and give him the money for it."

Jerome Burk, the sixth member of the group spoke up: "That there's more'n what he was askin."

"I know," Joseph agreed. "Mort will pay us all back for the extra out of his pay."

"I will?" Mort asked, surprised.

"Yes, you will." Henry said.

"Why do we all have to buy the pot?" Robert asked.

"'Cause we're all gonna eat out of it," Joseph answered. "And Mort will carry the pot when we ship out," he added. "Call it punishment for bringing a stolen pot to our fire." Joseph looked over at Henry.

The older brother remained silent but gave Joseph a nod.

"Then it's settled." Joseph pointed at the pot. "Get the water boiling and toss in the hardtack to boil out the weevils and maggots. I'm starving but not that starving." He leaned back and opened his diary again, then reached into his pocket and fished out his pencil. When he saw that the tip was dull, he clucked his tongue and handed the pencil over to Jerome.

Jerome pulled out a knife and began working the tip. He blew on it and handed it back. "You gonna write all this into your book?" he asked.

"No. Just a couple of lines about the day." Joseph smiled. "I'll put in that we all bought a pot."

"You still gonna write that letter for me to my wife?" Ash asked quietly.

"I can do it right now if you've a mind."

Ash looked around at the others and shook his head. "Later will be fine."

Joseph nodded and went back to his diary. When he'd finished writing, he wound the leather string around the cover and tucked it back into his tunic, then watched as Robert and Mort struggled to make a tripod out of branches to hang the pot over the fire. Jerome was trying to direct them with gestures, while Henry laughed every time the whole thing fell over. Even Ash seemed to take an interest.

Joseph shook his head and smiled. "Guess some things were just meant to be," he said quietly and moved to help with the tripod.

It took an hour to bring the meats, hardtack, and potatoes from their own rations to boil, and by then everyone was hovering greedily over the pot, their tin cups and spoons ready. Robert did the honors and doled out measured portions to, first, his companions, then himself.

Joseph sniffed the stew and his mouth began to water. Despite the saltpeter used to preserve the beef, the boiling had managed to make the meat somewhat tender and easier to eat. Even the hardtack, usually hard enough to break a tooth, had swollen into some semblance of dumplings. The soldiers sat in silence, each man savoring every spoonful. After their meal, they sat around the fire, watching the flames, their bellies full.

Mort began wiping his bugle down with a rag, while his brother sat next to him, picking his teeth.

Joseph burped. "Worth the dollar," he said.

There was a murmur of agreement around the fire.

"I was runnin' a message to the old man," Henry commented.

Joseph sat up and looked at the others. "What did it say?"

Henry barked out a laugh. "You forget I can't read past my own name. Why do you think they use me fer runnin' 'em?"

"Sorry," Joseph said, somewhat disappointed.

Henry waved him off. "I may not read and write, but I got

ears." He leaned back, smiling. Everyone was absolutely still as they waited for Henry to continue. "And I can hear a cricket burp a mile off."

Joseph looked around to see if anyone not from their group was nearby. If an officer happened by and heard, then Henry and maybe all of them could end up riding the "wooden mule." Joseph had seen a soldier ride the mule. The soldier was tied to a thin wooden rail for hours, his feet dangling on either side. Joseph shuddered at the memory.

"Robert," Joseph whispered, "keep a sharp eye out for officers."

The young man got up and moved to a place just outside the circle, but not so far that he couldn't hear what Henry had to say.

"You gonna sit there grinnin', or you gonna tell us?" Joseph whispered when he thought it was safe enough.

Henry dropped his grin and leaned toward the fire. Everyone in the circle followed suit.

"Seems things aren't goin' so well fer us," he said, his eyes darting around at the other men's faces.

"How so?" Mort asked.

"We lost some battles that were pretty important. The last one was at Lone Jack," Henry answered. "We lost an important commander, from what they was sayin'."

Joseph scratched his chin, in thought.

"What ya thinkin', Joseph?" Robert asked from behind.

"I'm thinkin' you best keep yer eyes peeled," Joseph shot back. He looked at Henry. "You heard right?" he asked.

"Seems to me like they'll want to put us into it, and do it soon."

"That's what I'm a-thinkin'."

"Did they talk about that?" Joseph asked.

"Some," Henry answered. "But nothing was said as to when or where."

Joseph straightened up and looked hard at the others. "It don't make no difference. It'll be soon enough, I reckon. Best we make the best of what drillin' is left and do it right."

The others murmured their agreement.

Joseph stood up to head to his roll, but stopped when he heard Ash clear his throat. Joseph looked over at the older man, who was holding out a piece of paper and an envelope.

"Right," he breathed. He waved his hand for Ash to follow. "Come on. We'll find a place to sit in quiet."

Joseph moved out of the circle of light, with Ash close behind.

FRIDAY, AUGUST 29, 1862

THE MARCH SOUTH

Joseph sat next to the small fire, drinking what was left of the coffee ration. He drew the collar of his tunic up against the constant drizzle of the rain and tugged the peak of his forage cap lower. It had been raining steadily for the last couple of days, and everyone and everything was soaked. Even the mood of the camp was dampened. Soldiers scurried from tent to tent or huddled together over fires at their duty posts.

They had received word that at dawn's light of the next day, they would be moving out. The colonel had given the men without sentry duty or those doing extra duty as punishment a day's furlough, should they have family close by.

Robert was sleeping in the tent he shared with Joseph, and

the Tinnerman brothers had gone off to try and get extra socks from the quartermaster shack. Joseph remembered the extra pairs he had bought at the mercantile the month before, and Jacob's face suddenly popped into his mind.

Joseph tossed what was left of the coffee on the ground and stood up. He'd heard that Jacob had been moved to D Company a couple of weeks ago to fill their ranks. Disease and injuries plagued all the companies, but D company seemed to take the brunt, and their ranks had been decimated by a run of dysentery. He began making his way between the rows of tents to find the man he had befriended in Little Falls.

It took the better part of an hour for Joseph to find the signpost designating the area as D Company, and he began looking for Jacob. He stopped a corporal, who pointed out a cluster of tents near the edge of the camp.

Joseph found his friend under a makeshift lean-to of oilcloth and branches. There was a small fire burning, and Jacob was sitting on a stump, staring at the flames as if deep in thought.

Joseph stood a couple of feet away and watched in silence, not sure if he should interrupt the man's thoughts or just leave quietly. His eyes followed Jacob's to the fire.

"You gonna sit for a bit or just stand there?"

Joseph glanced up from the fire and found Jacob gazing at him, a small smile on his face. "You looked like you were doing some hard thinkin'," Joseph explained. He grabbed another stump that lay in the grass and stood it on end near the fire so he could sit down.

"Was thinkin' 'bout my wife and son. Mostly about my son."

Joseph didn't know what to say.

"You want some coffee?" Jacob asked.

"Sure."

Jacob got up, went to the nearest tent, and stuck his head in. Joseph could hear him talking to someone inside, and moments later he emerged, carrying two tins filled with the steaming black liquid. He handed one to Joseph and sat down.

"Thank you." Joseph sipped the coffee, his mouth puckering slightly at the bitter taste.

"Not the best, I know."

Joseph smiled. "No worse than what we're serving."

The two men sat in silence, watching the muted movements of the camp.

"So the move south comes," Joseph said quietly. He laced his fingers around the tin cup.

"It comes," Jacob agreed.

"Are you ready?"

Jacob shrugged. "As ready as anyone else, I guess. If 'ready' is what you call it."

Joseph looked at the sea of tents spread out before them. "It's like waitin' for a storm you know is comin'." He took another sip.

"Waitin' for the storm is one thing," Jacob said. "The storm is already upon us." He tossed what was left of his coffee away. "And we're gonna be marchin' right into it."

"I find myself prayin' a lot these days." Joseph took a final swallow and tossed his coffee away with a grimace.

"I prayed right up to the night my wife died." Jacob looked at his friend with the same sad eyes Joseph had first met in front of the mercantile the month before.

"You don't pray no more?"

Jacob thought for a moment. "It's just me now," he said at

last. "Don't seem right to pray for me. Besides, if'n God says it's my time, then it's my time. I'll get to see my wife and boy again."

Joseph nodded. "Tell you what: I'll make you a bargain. I'll pray for you and you pray for me."

That brought a genuine smile to Jacob's lips. "I guess that'll do fine enough."

Joseph got to his feet and held out his hand. "I don't reckon we'll get to see much of each other before this is over."

Jacob stood too and took the younger man's hand warmly. "You stay alive, Joseph Hoover."

"You too, Jacob." He let the older man's hand go and turned away.

"I still haven't worn them socks," Jacob called out. "You want 'em back?"

Joseph turned back and smiled. "No. Deal's a deal," he said and continued on.

"Fair 'nough," Jacob called after him.

Joseph spent most of the afternoon wandering around the camp, in no hurry to get back to his tent. He watched as some soldiers lined up outside the building they had constructed to serve as the camp hospital, wondering what ailments they could have. They seemed healthy enough to his eyes, some smoking pipes and laughing with the next man, and others explaining why their leg hurt or their arm wouldn't do what it was supposed to. He shook his head and continued on.

The clouds still shrouded the sun, but the rain had finally stopped. The day's light was fading when he finally found the area he had called home for a month. The others had returned, and even Robert had emerged from the tent to sit around the fire.

"We were wondering when you would show up," Robert said with a grin. "Thought maybe you had deserted."

Joseph smiled. "Not before you, kid." He looked up at the darkening sky and could see breaks starting in the cloud cover. "Thinkin' the rain's done."

Ash looked up and nodded. "We might want to hang up these wet clothes we've been wearing. Let the fire dry them."

"That's a fine idea," Henry said. "We can string a rope near the fire." He pulled at his tunic and the shirt underneath. "Everything's stickin' to my skin." He got to his feet and began unbuttoning his tunic.

The others joined in, and soon they were standing around in their long underwear.

Robert and Mort strung a length of rope between two of the trees and began hanging their clothes.

"Rope's too close to the fire," Joseph said.

Mort eyed the rope and the clothes hanging from it. "It ain't."

"It's too close," Henry added.

Mort made a face. "I'm sayin' it ain't." He scowled at his older brother.

"Then why is your shirt on fire?" Henry pointed.

Mort let out a yell and grabbed his smoldering shirt and tossed it on the ground. He and Robert began stomping on the shirt while the rest laughed.

Mort lifted the shirt and squinted at it. The material was blackened along one side; the rest was covered in mud.

"Give it a wash," Robert suggested. "It'll be okay."

"I guess." Mort looked visibly upset.

"Come," said Joseph. "We can make our supper while the clothes dry. I don't know about the rest of you, but I'm hungrier than a bear."

The group spent the rest of the evening making their supper and talking about the march south. By the time they headed for their tents, the crescent moon had risen high in the starry night sky.

Joseph lay with his hands behind his head, staring at the stars through the open tent flap.

"What you doin', Joseph?" Robert asked.

"Lookin' and thinkin'."

"Whatcha lookin' at?"

"The stars."

"Huh." Robert turned on his back and looked out the tent flap at the stars. "Whatcha thinkin' 'bout?"

"Tomorrow."

"How do you think all this will end?" Robert asked.

"I don't know," Joseph answered. "I don't reckon we're supposed to know." He turned his head to look at Robert. "You worried?"

"Some. The stories we been hearing lately. They say it's not going so good for us." Robert took a deep breath. "Are you afraid, Joseph?"

Joseph caught the fear in the other man's voice. "Yes," he answered. "I think any man that says he ain't afraid ain't tellin' the truth."

"I guess."

"Best get some sleep, Robert. Tomorrow is going to be a long march."

"Yeah." Robert took another deep breath. "I'm afraid too."

"I know. Good night, Robert."

"Good night, Joseph."

SUNDAY, SEPTEMBER 14, 1862

BATTLE OF CRAMPTON'S GAP

Joseph stood in rank, looking out over the field his platoon would have to cross to reach the enemy line. Robert stood to his right, his youthful face streaked with dust and sweat. Ash stood to Robert's right, and Jerome and Henry had taken up positions almost directly behind them. Everyone was breathing hard.

They had broken camp at dawn and quick-marched for the whole morning, stopping only to eat a quick meal before taking to the road again. The colonel had ridden at the head of the column while the lieutenants rode their horses up and down the line, urging the men on. The sergeants kept their place at the head of each platoon, calling out the cadence in time with the drummers.

It wasn't until midafternoon that they reached Burkittsville and were told to hold position at the edge of a collection of buildings on the north side of the town.

Joseph looked out at the fields, and his breath left him. All the training, all the stories from other soldiers, did little to prepare him for what he now saw. Cannon fire from the ridge sent fountains of earth and grass rocketing into the air. The vibrations from the concussions traveled up his boots and into his chest. He watched as explosions erupted in the middle of platoons, sending men and body parts flying through the air. The cries and moans of the wounded, almost as loud as the roar of the cannons, shook him visibly.

Joseph watched as their own artillery began returning fire on the Confederate positions on the rise and in the gap. He took no pleasure in seeing men in gray uniforms suffering the same fate as his fellow soldiers.

"Oh, my sweet Lord, Joseph." Robert stood next to Joseph and shook his head. Tears streamed down his face.

"Steady, Robert." Joseph said. He looked up and down his own line and saw the same look of fear and disbelief on the rest of his platoon's faces.

The sergeant strode up to the front of the platoon and ordered them to attention. He was shouting louder than Joseph had ever heard him shout before as he tried to tell them what they were going to do. He finally gave up in frustration and waved the men to follow him.

Joseph slid his rifle off his shoulder and held it in front in the port arms position, the other men following his lead. The platoon quick-marched across a road that separated the town from the field and began to weave around other companies and platoons as they raced to find their position. Cannons exploded around them, but they managed to clear half the field without losing anyone.

A company formed ranks near the left flank of the Union forces, and from that position Joseph could see the Confederate guns dug in on the slopes just south of the gap. From his vantage point it looked as if the guns were pointed directly at him, and he had to force himself to keep from ducking every time one of the cannons fired.

He could hear the high-pitched screech of the balls as they passed by overhead or to the right and left, some landing so close he could feel the force of the blast on his back.

The explosions were taking their toll on Robert. He began shaking, and Joseph could hear small, almost whimpering sounds coming from the young man. Joseph reached over and took hold of Robert's left elbow.

"We're all scared," Joseph said. "When they give the order to advance, you stick close. You hear?"

Robert just nodded.

Henry "Joseph," Henry called from behind. "Can you see my brother?"

Joseph scanned the area and spotted Mort standing next to the colonel, his bugle held at the ready.

"He's up ahead," Joseph called back. "Standing next to the old man."

"Thank you."

The sergeant turned and bellowed at them. "Load your rifles, boys."

Joseph planted the butt of his rifle on the ground and began the motions to load his weapon. He mentally went through the count as he had done a hundred times in training: *Retrieve cartridge, tear cartridge, and pour powder into muzzle, fit mini ball into muzzle, grab ramrod, ram mini ball down barrel, slide ramrod back, half cock hammer, retrieve percussion cap and place on nipple.*

Joseph stood with his rifle held at the port arms position and waited. Soon everyone in the platoon was standing ready.

The sergeant took a look at the men and bobbed his head. He spun around and stood in front of the platoon, waiting for the command to advance.

Joseph stood still, his eyes traveling over the battlefield, watching as other platoons also stood at the ready.

"When do you think they'll send us in?" Robert asked.

"Soon, I reckon." Joseph nodded toward the colonel and saw the old man signal to Mort, who put the bugle to his lips and blew the command to advance.

The front ranks of soldiers began a slow march eastward across the field toward the road and fence line that marked the base of the rise.

"God keep you safe, men, and make your aim true," the sergeant called back. He stiffened his back and bellowed the command, "Platoon, by the left, MARCH!"

The training that had been drilled into them took over, and the platoon advanced as one, each soldier stepping forward with his left foot as they began. That simple act gave Joseph a sense of pride, and he gripped his rifle tighter as he followed behind the sergeant.

They marched for about a hundred yards without drawing any fire from the enemy, but as they neared the road, Joseph could hear bullets whining past their heads and see the ground erupt in small explosions in front.

"When are we going to fire back?" Robert asked nervously. He began to flinch as bullets hit the ground nearby.

Sarg✓ "Steady," the sergeant called out. "We are still several hundred yards away. No need to waste shot."

Robert "Doesn't seem to bother the enemy."

Sarge "That's because they're a bunch of rebellious rabble. Not professional soldiers, such as yourself," the sergeant growled back.

The sergeant called for the men to halt just shy of the road. By then bullets were whizzing above their heads, making everyone flinch and duck. "Back row, half step to the left!" he roared.

The rear line stepped to the left so they were staggered from the front row.

"Front row, aim!"

Joseph raised his gun and sighted down the barrel at the men in Confederate uniforms standing around the cannon emplacement. He pulled the hammer to the full cock position and held his breath.

"Fire!"

Joseph pulled the trigger. He felt the kick of the recoil, smelled the smoke from the powder, and heard the loud rapport all in a split second. He knew that everyone in the front row had fired, but he could only remember what happened when he pulled the trigger on his own rifle.

Two of the Confederate soldiers working the cannons had fallen. Joseph had no idea if his shot had hit anything.

"Reload!" the sergeant shouted over the noise of the battlefield.

Joseph began to reload in earnest, his mind going over the counts.

"Second row, ready!"

The men in the second row raised their rifles over the shoulders of the men in the first row. Joseph could see a barrel out of the corner of his eye as he continued to reload his own weapon.

"Fire!"

Joseph's ear rang from the report, and he winced from the pain but ignored it. He rammed the mini ball down with his rod, lifted his rifle, and pulled the hammer to half cock. He felt a moment of panic as he fumbled a bit for the percussion cap before finally getting it placed on the gun's nipple.

He eyed the ridge where the cannons were and saw that several more soldiers had fallen.

"Forward, march!"

The platoon began moving at a slow march toward the road.

Joseph watched as the fallen soldiers were replaced and were now desperately trying to raise the rear of the cannons to bring the muzzle down to bear on their lines.

"Platoon, halt!" The sergeant turned his head to the side. "Front row, aim!

Joseph raised his rifle and carefully aimed at one of the soldiers.

"Fire!"

Joseph watched through the thin curtain of smoke as the soldier he had aimed at dropped to the ground.

"I think you got him, Joseph!" Robert yelled, a big grin splitting his face.

Joseph grimaced at what he had done. He dropped the butt of his rifle onto the ground and grabbed for another paper cartridge.

"Second line, aim! FIRE!"

Joseph turned the right side of his head away from the rifle barrel to try and lessen the pain in his ear. He managed to get another percussion cap onto the nipple before the cannons began firing.

The first round struck the ground behind them, but close enough for the force of the explosion to push the rear line forward. One man near the far left rear line screamed and fell to the ground. The second round fell far to the right of the platoon and exploded harmlessly.

Ash turned to Robert with a smile on his face. "Looks like we got 'em too scared to aim straight."

Both Joseph and Robert looked at Ash just as the third cannon roared. The cannonball took Ash square in the chest. Joseph watched in horror as Ash's face, still frozen in the smile, blurred and was gone.

Robert turned back to Joseph, his eyes wide and his face and chest covered in Ash's blood. He began to shake uncontrollably.

"Steady, men!" the sergeant called out. "Platoon, fire at will!"

Joseph raised his rifle and fired, not even taking time to aim. The rest of the platoon fired a round, but the men on the ridge had taken cover behind the cannons and were now returning fire.

A man on Joseph's left fell, his screams filling the air.

"Make for the fence!" The Sergeant ran forward, drawing the men after him.

Joseph grabbed Robert's coat and pulled him along as they raced across the road. Joseph pushed his friend down into the long grass at the fence before diving down himself. Bullets began hitting all around them, and they were showered with splinters of wood.

Robert's eyes were still wide with terror as he huddled on the ground, shaking.

"You have to reload, Robert!" Joseph grabbed Robert's arm and shook him. "Robert! We need to reload!"

Robert nodded and began fumbling for a cartridge. He dropped two on the ground, his hands shaking so bad that he could barely hold on to his rifle.

Joseph grabbed the front of Robert's coat and pulled him close. "Robert! Look at me!"

Robert's eyes darted to Joseph's face.

"We'll do it together," Joseph said, trying to calm his own voice. "Just like in drill." He rose up to his knees so he could get a sharper angle on the barrel.

"We're gonna die, Joseph!"

"No, we ain't! Now, get up!"

Robert managed to get to his knees.

"Keep looking at me!" Joseph yelled above the gunfire. Bullets still whined around them, but Joseph ignored everything except for Robert. "Pick up a cartridge!"

Robert grabbed one of the dropped cartridges.

Joseph reached into his pouch and pulled out one of his own. "Do what I do!" He tore the cartridge open with his teeth, watching Robert do the same. He poured the powder down the barrel and waited while Robert did the same thing. Joseph pushed the mini ball into the end of the barrel with his thumb, making sure that Robert followed his motions. Joseph could see that Robert was slowly getting control of his actions and his shaking had lessened. Each rammed the bullet down and replaced the ramrod to its holder.

By the time they had replaced the percussion caps, Joseph

could see that Robert had lost the look of panic in his face.

"Fix bayonets!" the sergeant yelled as he pulled out his own bayonet.

A panicked expression returned to Robert's face, but Joseph put a hand on the young man's shoulder and squeezed. "We'll get through this," he whispered fiercely. "Just follow me."

They both pulled out their bayonets and jammed them down on the end of their rifles.

Joseph looked up and down the fence line. Union soldiers were packed against the fence as far as he could see. Joseph felt a wave of adrenaline course through his veins at the thought of that many men charging up the slope. He gripped his rifle tighter, waiting for the command.

A bugle sounded, and Joseph knew that Mort was somewhere in the line, blowing as hard as he could.

The sergeant raised his rifle up. "Charge!"

The command was repeated up and down the line as the Union soldiers rose up and over the fence.

Joseph pulled himself over the top rail and reached around and yanked Robert after him. He turned up the slope and began running, his rifle held waist high.

The Confederate soldiers near the cannons began firing. Soldiers to Joseph's left began falling, and he doubled his efforts to reach the position before the enemy could reload.

He risked a quick look to his right and saw Robert keeping pace.

They closed on the position and Joseph raised his rifle and pulled the trigger as some of the Confederate soldiers rose up to fire on them.

Union soldiers up and down the line began firing as they

charged, causing the Confederate soldiers to turn and run.

A yell rose from the Union ranks, and Joseph found himself screaming at the top of his lungs as he leapt over the low earthen berm and past the now silent cannons.

A group of Confederate soldiers turned and held their ground, their rifles with bayonets poised dangerously in front.

Joseph reached the line. One of the Confederate soldiers charged him, and he barely managed to sweep the man's rifle aside before plunging his bayonet into his attacker's chest. There was a sickening crunch as the blade drove past the bones of the rib cage and Joseph had to swallow hard to keep from vomiting. Beside him, Robert hesitated, and another soldier batted Robert's rifle to the side.

Joseph watched as Robert fell back and the Confederate soldier raised his weapon to drive the bayonet into his friend. Joseph dropped his rifle and launched his body at the man. His weight caught the enemy off balance, and they fell to the ground. The two grappled in the dirt like boys fighting over an insult.

The soldier managed to get on top of Joseph and wrap his hands around Joseph's throat. He began squeezing the breath from him.

Just as Joseph's vision began to blur, he saw Robert looming over the soldier. He watched as Robert brought the butt of his rifle down hard on the side of the man's head.

It took Joseph a minute to catch his breath before rolling the unconscious soldier off. He got to his feet and nodded his thanks to Robert.

"Looks like we got 'em on the run," Robert said.

Joseph turned and saw a wave of blue uniforms rolling over the crest of the ridge, driving the Confederates into the gap.

WILLIAM R. WALTERS & MICHAEL DAVIS

"Looks like," he said. He looked around and saw his rifle. He picked it up and began loading it. "Reckon we should join 'em." He finished reloading and started up the slope at a jog, Robert close on his heels.

They reached the gap and saw that the Confederates had completely broken ranks and were running wildly away from the Union charge. Joseph and Robert had already started down the other side of the gap when they heard the bugle recalling the soldiers.

"Why are we stopping?" Robert asked.

Joseph shook his head. "Don't rightly know." He shouldered his rifle and waved for Robert to follow. "Let's go find the others."

They wandered through the milling soldiers until Robert spotted Mort. He was standing alone with his bugle held against his chest. Mort saw Robert and gave a wave.

"What happened?" Joseph asked when they met.

"Dunno," Mort answered. "The general ordered the old man to recall the soldiers."

"No reason why?"

Mort shook his head. "The old man tells me what to blow and I blow." He looked around with a worried look on his face. "Have you seen Henry? I been lookin' for him, but the whole platoon is scattered."

"We have not seen anyone since we charged the cannons," Joseph answered. "I am sure he is well."

"We're going to go look for the others," Robert said. "Come with us."

Mort shook his head again. "The old man ordered me to stay here in case he needed to find me."

"Then we will find him and bring him here." Joseph looked at the valley below and pointed at large group of Union soldiers standing around, waiting for a command. "We can start there."

It took the better part of an hour before they found Henry and Jerome. They had stayed together during the charge against the cannons and after following the army through the gap. Henry spotted Joseph and called out to him.

Joseph saw a bloody bandage on Henry's left arm.

"It's just a scratch," Henry said with a shrug. "Confederate officer tried to stick me with his sword." He tilted his head at Jerome. "Jerome got him from behind."

"You should get the surgeon to look at that," Joseph said.

"Later. The surgeons have their hands full with worse." He looked past Joseph and Robert. "Have you seen Mort?"

Joseph turned and pointed up the slope to a single figure. "He's waiting up there." He turned and looked at the soldiers in the valley. "We might as well go wait with Mort. He'll probably know what is going to happen before anyone else."

They began walking back up the slope toward Mort.

"Ash?" Jerome asked.

"Gone," Joseph answered quietly.

They reached Mort and the two brothers hugged hard.

"Any word on what we are doing?"

Mort shrugged his shoulders.

At that moment a runner arrived, breathing hard. "The old man says we camp in the valley tonight," he said, and left at a run.

Mort put the bugle to his lips and blew the call that would tell the soldiers in the vicinity to make camp.

"Well, let's find a spot to settle in for the night."

Jerome "I shared my half tent with Ash," Jerome said.

Joseph sighed. "Come. We'll find a decent spot and worry about that later."

They walked around until they found a spot under a large oak and made camp. Jerome wandered off on his own while the others set up their tents and gathered wood for the fire. By the time they had a fire going, Jerome had returned with another soldier. He introduced the young soldier to everyone.

Jerome "This is Thomas," he said. "He's from the Eighteenth New York."

"You lose your tent half?" Joseph asked.

Thomas "Yeah," answered Thomas. "He took a bullet almost at the start of the battle."

Robert made room for Thomas to sit on the ground.

Jerome "Anyone feel like eating?" Jerome asked.

A chorus of nos came from the group.

Joseph took out his diary and flipped to the back of the book. He took great pains to remove the last blank page, making sure it didn't tear.

Robert "You not gonna write about today?" Robert asked.

Joseph "Later," Joseph said. "I thought I'd write to Ash's family first."

Mort "The army will do that," Mort said.

Joseph "Yeah, I know." Joseph took out his pencil and licked the point. "But the army don't <u>know</u> Ash. <u>We</u> do."

"It's right that you do it," agreed Henry. "We'll all sign our names when you're done."

Joseph settled into a better position and began writing the letter.

5

WEDNESDAY, DECEMBER 10, 1862

EVE OF THE BATTLE OF FREDERICKSBURG

"I can't believe how cold it is!" Joseph complained as he and Robert made their way back to their small campsite. Both of them carried canvas sacks full of provisions to make a half-decent stew to help ward off the cold.

"At least we got most of what we need," Robert answered, his breath creating small swirls of mist as he spoke. "I can't wait to eat."

The last week had been hard on everyone as they quick-marched across the state to join up with the rest of the army on the east banks of the Rappahannock. They had moved so fast that the supply wagons for the regiment had been left far behind, and even though they had arrived at the camp the previous evening, they were left to scrounge food wherever they could.

Both Joseph and Henry had been against ranging out into the countryside to forage food from the local farms, forcing them instead to go from campsite to campsite, bartering and in some cases begging for supplies. Most had told them to move on, but it was a large encampment, and eventually they found soldiers willing to part with some salted pork or the odd potato. Many were willing to give their hardtack away for free.

"Let's hope the others had good luck." Joseph pointed to a familiar cluster of pine trees. "Looks like they got a fire going."

"Good," Robert said with a shiver. "I'm froze right down to my bones."

Mort saw the two approach and raised his hand in greeting. He was busy stirring something in the pot.

"What have you got in the pot?" Joseph asked, tossing his sack on the ground next to the fire.

"Bits of beef we got from some fellers with the Eighty-second." Mort answered. He bent over the pot and frowned. "At least they said it was beef."

Joseph peered into the pot. "Looks more like possum."

Mort shrugged. "Possum is okay by me." He looked at the sack on the ground and the one that Robert was still holding. "What did you bring?"

"We got salted pork," Robert said, opening his sack. "Some potatoes, couple of carrots, and lots of hardtack."

"Give it here and I'll cut it up for the pot."

Robert handed his sack to Mort and sat down.

Henry was sitting on a thick log they had found the night before and dragged to the fire. Joseph sat down next to him and rubbed his hands over the fire. "How goes it, Henry?"

Henry "Dunno, really." Henry spat into the fire. "That new colonel we got seems decent enough."

Joseph "But?" Joseph asked, catching a tone in the other's voice.

Henry "He's awful young, Joseph."

Joseph sighed and stared up at the evening sky. "What's the lieutenant say about him?"

Henry shook his head. "Nothin' in front of me."

Joseph "Well," Joseph said, rubbing his beard. "I reckon it won't matter much come the morrow. There's a hundred thousand and more of us for the battle. I expect there'll be more colonels and generals shoutin' orders and pointin'. Figure at least one of them's going to get it right."

Henry "You'd think," Henry said.

Jerome "Did you find your friend?" Jerome asked.

Joseph shook his head. "I haven't seen Jacob since the day before Crampton's Gap. I'm not even sure he survived the battle." He frowned at the thought and stared at the flames.

Robert "Supper will be ready soon," Robert said, changing the subject.

Henry looked in the pot and made a clucking sound. "Throw a handful of flour in. Thicken the gravy so it sticks to our ribs."

Robert "Don't got any," Robert answered.

Joseph "It'll do," said Joseph. He looked around the circle, trying to memorize what each man looked like. He thought of Ash and found it hard to remember his face. Try as he might, he could only recall what Ash's face had looked like the moment he died.

Mort "What do you think tomorrow will be like?" Mort asked his older brother.

Henry Henry shrugged. "Crowded is mostly what I'm thinkin'."

43

"Best not to dwell on it," Joseph said. "It'll be morning soon enough. We don't need to rush it."

"I'll agree to that." Henry gave Joseph a nudge. "The camp over yonder"—he pointed a finger at another clump of tents—"they got a decent game of cards going. You want to head over and test our luck?"

Joseph shook his head. "Don't got any money."

"Why not?" Henry asked, surprised. "We got some of our pay from the paymaster before we set out."

"Sent it home," Joseph said. He pulled out the leather-bound diary and started flipping through the pages.

"I'll spot you a couple of greenbacks," Henry urged. "We might make enough to pay for some better victuals than what we got."

"Or we could lose it all," Joseph countered.

Henry jabbed his thumb at his chest. "I'm what you'd call a pretty good gambler."

"No such thing as a good gambler." Joseph looked up from the diary. "Like as not, we'll end up broke and I'll end up owing you."

"What if we win?"

There was a loud shout from the group of tents where the game was on. The shout was followed by cursing and what sounded like a fistfight.

"Something tells me winnin' with that group would be worse than losing." Joseph turned his attention back to his diary.

Henry frowned and let the matter drop.

Robert tapped the side of the pot with his tin plate. "Food's ready."

Joseph closed the diary and shoved it back into his overcoat.

"'Bout time. My stomach's growlin' like a bear."

"Was wondering what that noise was." Jerome smiled and handed Robert his cup. "Fill 'er up."

Joseph lay on his back, rolled in his blanket. He had decided to bed down almost as soon as he had finished eating. He stared at the oiled canvas above his head, thinking about what would come with the new day. The others were still talking about tomorrow's battle, but even though it was all he could think about, Joseph did not feel like sharing his thoughts.

He wondered how Jacob was doing and if he was even alive. He said a prayer for his friend, as he had promised, and then said another one for his family back home. He thought about what they would be doing now. The crops would be in, and they would be getting the farm ready for winter. He thought about the last letter he had received from them. It had been dated the day he had mustered out.

He smiled as he thought about the doings of his brothers and sisters and talk about the crops almost ready to come in. He knew his absence would be felt during the harvest, but sending his pay home had helped, and they were going to hire a hand to help in his place. There had been talk about the lists of those dead, injured, and missing and how many of the local young men were on it.

Joseph frowned at the thought of his mother going over the lists, looking for his own name. He promised to write another letter tomorrow night.

The tent shook as Robert entered and dropped on his blanket next to him.

"Everyone calling it a night?" Joseph asked.

Robert "Henry's gone to the next camp to try his luck, but the rest have turned in," Robert answered. He rolled himself in his blanket and lay on his side, facing Joseph.

Joseph "Something on your mind?" Joseph asked.

Robert "I'm worried about tomorrow."

Joseph "You're not alone, Robert. I'm guessing everyone, on both sides, is thinkin' the same thing."

Robert "I'm worried that I'll do the same as Crampton's Gap."

Joseph turned his head so he could see Robert. "You did fine, Robert."

Robert "When Ash—" Robert stopped for a moment and took a breath. "When he got hit . . . I ain't never seen anything like that. If you hadn't been there, I reckon I'd still be there, froze to the ground." It was the first time since the battle of the gap that Robert had talked about what had happened.

Joseph "You got hold of yourself quick enough."

Henry "Only 'cause you were there," Robert argued. "What if the same thing happens tomorrow?"

Joseph shook his head. "I ain't gonna tell you it won't. But you got hold of your wits and saved my hide when that Confederate was choking the life out of me."

Robert smiled. "You were turning a right shade of blue."

Joseph chuckled. "I'll have to take your word for it."

They stopped talking for a bit.

Robert "It was good stew tonight," Robert said quietly.

Joseph "It was."

Robert "You think tomorrow will end all of this?"

Joseph shook his head. "I can't say, Robert. Most we can do is pray it'll end."

Robert "I reckon."

"Best get some sleep," Joseph said.

"Yeah."

Joseph closed his eyes, but it was a long time before he finally found sleep.

6

THURSDAY, DECEMBER 11, 1862

BRIDGING THE RAPPAHANNOCK RIVER

Joseph stood in rank, watching the army engineers make attempt after attempt to build the pontoon bridges that would carry the army across the Rappahannock to the west bank. Confederate sharpshooters and cannon hit the unprotected soldiers again and again, causing them to retreat.

The carnage had started just before dawn, and despite heavy shelling of the town and west bank by the Union Army, the Confederates held their ground and continued to pour withering sniper fire into the men wrestling with the huge sections of the floating bridges.

Henry "They're gettin' cut down hard, Joseph." Henry was in the second line, behind Joseph.

Joseph "I know it," Joseph said.

Robert "It ain't fair," Robert whispered. "Us standing here half-cocked and them getting shot up like that."

Joseph "Fair's got nothin' to do with it," Joseph whispered fiercely back. "We got our job, they got theirs."

Robert shook his head. "That's cold, Joseph."

"I got eyes same as you," Joseph shot back. "I can see what's goin' on." He gripped his rifle to his chest. "Ain't nothin' I want more than to charge down there and do some shootin' back." He looked over to the spot where the colonel sat on his horse, his gaze moving over the banks of the river. "Until the colonel says different, we stand here and wait."

Joseph saw movement out of the corner of his eye and turned his face south. Several companies had made their way across the river on pontoon boats and were moving on the Confederate sniper positions.

Joseph "See there," he called to the others and pointed with the muzzle of his rifle. "They got a plan; make no mistake."

They all watched as the Union soldiers began firing and running up the bank. Several Confederate soldiers left their positions and began retreating before the others could reach them.

"Ha!" Robert called out. "They put 'em on the run!"

Joseph smiled. "At least those poor men can finish the bridges."

Henry "You think we'll cross today?" Henry asked.

Joseph looked at the sun. It had already passed its zenith and was heading west, causing their shadows to stretch out on the cold ground. "They ain't got but a few hours of daylight left. I <u>don't</u> reckon the generals will want to risk a night crossing."

There was a murmuring of agreement from the platoon.

They spent the rest of the day standing like silent sentinels while the bridges slowly grew toward the west bank of the river.

The sun had nearly set when the buglers sounded the call to make camp for the night.

Robert "So we cross tomorrow?" Robert asked as they broke ranks.

Joseph "Looks like," Joseph answered. "Come on. Let's see if we can't find a half decent place to pitch our tents."

7

FRIDAY, DECEMBER 12, 1862

THE STREETS OF FREDERICKSBURG

Joseph knelt at the end of the pontoon bridge his company had been assigned to cross. The platoon crowded in behind him, waiting for the signal to cross. He felt the adrenaline coursing through his veins, and his heart was beating so hard he could feel it pounding in his chest. Despite the coolness of the December morning, he was sweating profusely.

Upstream, Joseph could see wave after wave of Union soldiers sprinting across another bridge, some falling into the river after being hit by sniper fire.

"I thought they got rid of the snipers!" Robert yelled over the noise of gunfire and the shouted commands from officers kneeling on the bridge.

"I'm guessing they missed a few," Joseph said.

Everyone ducked as bullets hit the water nearby.

"Why are we waiting here?" Henry asked.

"We have to wait until the others clear the far end of the bridge." Joseph looked to the sergeant kneeling a few feet away. "What about it, Sarge?"

The sergeant glanced over at the lieutenant and spat into the water. He turned back to Joseph. "We wait."

Just then the lieutenant stood up. "Sergeant, move the men across!"

"You heard the man," the sergeant said. "Form up in twos!"

Joseph pushed off the ground and stood with his rifle at the ready. Robert took his position to Joseph's right. The two men exchanged a quick glance and nod.

The sergeant leaned over and checked the line, making sure everyone was ready. "Forward, quick-march! Remember to break step!"

Joseph and Robert moved forward quickly, following the sergeant across the wooden planks that were stretched across the pontoons. Joseph soon realized that even if the command to break step had not been issued, it would have been nearly impossible to march in unison with the decking bouncing and moving from side to side. The two men bounced off each other a dozen or so times as they crossed.

Despite the danger, Robert began laughing and even Joseph was grinning by the time they reached the far bank. They moved quickly up the short slope and took cover behind a stone wall. "I reckon any sniper trying to make bead on us would be seasick by now," Robert laughed. A mini ball ricocheted off the top of the wall, and he crouched down even lower.

Joseph "I reckon." Joseph smiled at the thought of seasick Confederates.

& Henry "That was the craziest run I ever been on!" Henry said as he dove for cover next to Joseph.

The sergeant moved along the wall until he was squatting next to Robert. "We'll move into the town along that street yonder," he said, pointing to their left.

Joseph chanced a peek over the wall and saw what looked more like an alleyway than a street. "Not much room to spread out, Sergeant. We get caught in there, it'll be like shootin' fish in a barrel for 'em."

Sarge "I know," the sergeant answered. "But those are the orders, and we <u>follow</u> orders." He checked up and down the fence and saw that everyone from the platoon had cleared the bridge.

Sarge "We'll go house to house making sure no Confederates are hiding." He found the lieutenant at the end of the line of men and saw the signal. "Right. Let's get this over with." He rose up and climbed over the short wall. "Follow me, boys!"

INTENSE. The whole platoon rose and started over the wall. Two men fell as soon as they stood up. One clutched at his stomach before falling backward onto the bank; the other man dropped like a stone, the back of his head blown away.

Joseph followed close on the sergeant's heels as they made their way to the line of buildings next to the entrance of the street.

The sergeant waved for half the platoon to cross the entrance and take up positions on the other side. Once everyone was in position, the sergeant led the men into the street.

The platoon formed two lines on either side, keeping close to the buildings. They moved slow, eyes constantly lifting to the windows above them.

Joseph came to a door and stopped. He tried the handle and it turned. He swung the door open and peered into the dark interior. He cocked his head to Robert, letting him know to follow.

Then both entered and Joseph stopped just inside to let his eyes adjust to the dim light.

Robert tapped him on the shoulder and pointed at an oil lamp on a small table.

Joseph shook his head. "Give 'em somethin' to shoot at," he whispered. He moved forward, holding his rifle upright so it wouldn't bang into anything. Joseph reached a doorway and tilted his head around the jamb. He motioned for Robert to follow as he moved into the next room.

A set of stairs led to the second floor, and Joseph crept to the foot, his eyes searching the stairwell above. He froze when he heard a creaking noise just above their heads.

Joseph took a step back and slung his rifle across his shoulders so he would have both his hands free. He took out his bayonet and held it low as he returned to the bottom step and began to climb.

Joseph reached the halfway point and suddenly leapt backward. There was the loud crack of a rifle going off and the tread he had been standing on splintered from a bullet striking the wood.

Joseph yelled at the top of his lungs and raced up the steps two at a time.

The sudden charge took Robert off guard, and he struggled to follow his friend up the stairs. He turned the landing just in time to see Joseph grappling with a Confederate soldier.

Joseph pushed the soldier back and plunged his bayonet into the man's chest as they both fell to the floor. Joseph lay on top of the man, his breath coming in gasps. He pushed himself off and leaned against the stair railing as he fought to get his breath back.

A door across from the stairs burst open and another soldier appeared, his rifle aimed at Joseph. There was another loud crack, and the soldier fell back into the room dead.

Joseph looked at Robert and nodded.

"I thought you'd lost your mind," Robert said as he climbed the rest of the steps. He held his hand out to Joseph.

Joseph took the hand and let Robert pull him to his feet. "I was wonderin' that myself." He looked at the dead soldier he had stabbed. "I figured I could reach him before he had a chance to reload." He looked at the other soldier. "Never occurred to me there would be a second one."

"Just promise me you won't go runnin' off like that again." Robert dropped the butt of his rifle on the floor and began reloading.

"We should check the other rooms," Joseph said. He pulled his bayonet from the man's chest and wiped the blood off.

Robert finished reloading; then they cleared the rest of the floor and returned to the street. The rest of the platoon had moved several yards ahead, and they ran to catch up.

"Where did you two go?" Henry asked as he continued to scan the windows and doorways.

"We ran into a couple of soldiers in the first building," Robert answered.

"Take care of 'em?"

"One apiece," Joseph said. He looked up and down the street. "Come across any more?"

Henry shook his head. "Looks like they cleared out. The

sergeant says we'll move over one more street and check it out before we stop for the night."

Robert "We gonna sleep in one of the buildings?" Robert asked.

"Don't see why not," Joseph replied. "It'll be good to sleep on somethin' that ain't hard ground."

The platoon reached the end of the street and waited for the sergeant and lieutenant to decide which way they would go.

Before they could decide, Henry's younger brother came running up. He had to stop for a second to catch his breath before he delivered a written message to the lieutenant.

The lieutenant read the note before tucking it into his tunic. "Sergeant, lead the men south to the next street. Make sure it is free of enemy soldiers; then find a suitable building to bed down." He looked at the men as they stood in a semicircle around him. "There are reports of Union soldiers looting the town," he told them. "That is unacceptable. I find out anyone from this platoon has besmirched the honor of this command, I will have them shot."

Henry "What about food, sir?" Henry asked.

"The quartermaster should be setting up supply tents by now, but I'll allow foraging for foodstuffs."

"Very good, sir!" The sergeant saluted. "We'll not act in any manner other than a soldier should."

Lieut "I'll take your word for it, Sergeant." The lieutenant returned the salute and left.

The sergeant turned on the men. "You heard him. We are not thieves, brigands, or barbarians." He tilted his kepi and put his hands on his hips. "Having said that, the first man who brings me a decent cup of coffee doesn't have to stand watch."

The sergeant was met with smiles and muted laughter.

The sun hung heavy in the west by the time they had cleared the next street. The men found a building relatively undamaged by the cannon barrage and moved into it for the night.

The building had been a warehouse for cotton bales, and even though it was empty, there were piles of dirty and moldy cotton strewn about. Joseph collected an armload and found a corner of the main floor to lay his blanket down. He smoothed out the cotton, spread his blanket over it, and lay down with a sigh.

"Any luck finding some food?" Robert asked, setting his pack down and taking out his bedroll.

"Didn't look."

"Not hungry?"

"Starving," Joseph answered. "But I'm tired, and the thought of layin' down was stronger than eatin'."

"The others found a fireplace and managed to get a fire going," Robert said. "Might be warmer if we bed down there."

Joseph sighed again. He rolled onto his side and sat up. "I guess." He stood up and gathered his belongings and what cotton he could scoop up and followed his young friend.

They found the others huddled around the fireplace, their blankets wrapped around their shoulders. Joseph and Robert joined them.

"Anyone have any luck finding food?" Robert asked.

"Ain't bothered to look," Henry said.

"I still got some hardtack," Jerome offered. He reached into his haversack and pulled out a handful of the hard, square biscuits.

"We all still got hardtack," Mort grumbled.

"I'd rather have a cup of coffee." Joseph rummaged around

in his bag and pulled up a couple of handfuls of black coffee grounds. "Give the pot over," he told Mort.

Mort held the pot in front of Joseph, who dumped in both handfuls. Joseph managed to get another half a handful of coffee out of his sack. Mort left to go find water.

"Any news on tomorrow?" Joseph asked Henry.

Henry shook his head. "Mort said this whole mess was supposedly a surprise, but I reckon the surprise is gone now."

Joseph nodded his agreement. "Tomorrow will be the test."

Mort returned with the potful of water and set it down in the embers of the fireplace.

Everyone held their cups out after the coffee had boiled. Joseph breathed in the strong odor and closed his eyes. He took a sip. The coffee was strong and bitter but he welcomed it. He grabbed one of Jerome's hardtack biscuits and soaked one end in the coffee until it was soft enough to chew. Even the tasteless meal was welcome.

After finishing his coffee, he took out his diary and wrote a few lines before stretching out on the floor, his boots near the fire. He fell asleep as soon as he tucked his arm under his head.

8

SATURDAY, DECEMBER 13, 1862

BATTLE OF FREDERICKSBURG

Robert "Have you ever seen so many people in one place?" Robert asked, his voice awed by what he was seeing.

Joseph "No," Joseph answered. "Never."

Their platoon had quick-marched south from the city just before dawn and now stood with hundreds of other platoons, facing a rise they had been told was called Prospect Hill. Behind them, the Union gun emplacements on the Stafford Heights were sending a seemingly never-ending barrage of cannon fire on the Confederate positions all along the crest of the hill

Joseph looked at the ground they would have to cover to gain the hill, and he shook his head. There was little to provide cover, and they would be exposed for the better part of a mile while they advanced.

A shiver went up his back.

Henry "They say it's Stonewall Jackson on the hill." Henry grunted.

Robert "Stonewall?" Robert said. "That ain't good, is it, Joseph?"

Joseph "I don't think it matters much who is up there," Joseph said. He tried to get his guts to unwind at the thought. "Colonel says we gotta take that hill; then we take that hill."

Henry "It's going to be hard goin'," Henry said.

Joseph "In case you have forgot, this ain't a fall fair we're attendin'." Joseph was getting anxious with all the talk. "Keep your mouths shut and your eyes open. Look for places to take cover."

Robert "There ain't none, Joseph." There was a slight tremor of fear in Robert's voice.

Henry "They'll be plenty once the cannonballs start falling," said Henry.

Robert "When do you think it will start?" Robert asked.

Serge "You men will be in the second wave," the sergeant answered, coming up from behind the platoon. He moved to stand in front of the men. "Colonel Meade will lead the charge."

Bugles began sounding all around them.

Serge "You asked when it starts," the sergeant said to Robert. "It starts now. Make sure you're ready."

Joseph "He'll be fine, Sergeant," Joseph said. "We won't let you down."

The sergeant nodded and turned to face the enemy.

Joseph watched as the leading companies began moving forward. All along the line, farther than he could see, a wave of blue moved out from the town and along the west side of the river.

Just then the Confederate cannons began spitting their deadly ammunition at the advancing line of Union soldiers.

The air filled with shrapnel from cannonballs bursting over their heads or exploding in their midst.

All along the advancing tide, soldiers were dropping to the ground, most to lie still, others to writhe in agony from their wounds. The sight caught Joseph's breath as he watched the carnage unfold before him. It hardly seemed possible that the charge could continue, but slowly the army advanced against the constant barrage until it seemed to Joseph that they would reach the enemy lines. A shout went up from the soldiers around him, and he joined in urging the men on.

The front of the line moved to within a few hundred yards of the Confederates before they finally opened up with their rifles. The entire ridge disappeared in smoke as thousands of Confederate rifles fired at almost the same time.

Joseph and the others watched in horror as the entire front of the Union charge collapsed under the hail of bullets. The soldiers at the rear of the charge moved forward, and again the enemy rifles sounded and again the Union charge was stalled.

Men lay on the ground by the hundreds, and those not hit milled about the field in confusion as the Confederate soldiers continued to fire their muskets.

Slowly, the Union soldiers began to retreat down the slope while the rifle and cannon fire continued to wreak havoc among the ranks.

"Get ready, men," the sergeant said quietly.

"How are we going to get through that?" Henry asked.

"You keep moving forward. That's how you get through," the sergeant replied.

"What are we gonna do, Joseph?" Robert whispered.

"We're soldiers," Joseph answered. He swallowed hard to

keep his voice calm. "We keep moving forward." He looked out over the devastation of the battlefield, the bodies of those who had fallen, and did the only thing he could think of. "Yea, though I walk through the valley of the shadow of death, I will fear no evil: for thou art with me; thy rod and thy staff they comfort me."

There was a chorus of amens around him.

The bugle sounded again. The sergeant stiffened and yelled, "Platoon, march!"

Joseph, Robert, and the rest stepped off and followed the sergeant up the slope toward the Confederate position. The colonel strode along with the men, his saber pointed to the front.

The cannon fire started almost immediately. Air bursts showered the companies with red-hot bits of cast iron, felling soldiers by the dozen. Some of the balls exploded in the ground, blinding the men with dirt and sending others flying apart.

The colonel turned to the right suddenly and began a quick march up the gentle slope toward an area of thick wood and underbrush.

The Confederate cannons went silent as the crews fought to turn them but were quickly replaced with volleys of rifle fire from the underbrush.

Joseph realized that the gunfire was not as heavy as it had been along the other line.

"Platoons, halt! Prepare to fire!" The sergeant moved to the side as he yelled at the soldiers.

Joseph and Robert were in the first line, and they knelt on the ground and cocked their weapons. The second and third lines remained standing and staggered their positions so each could fire with a clear line of sight.

Sarge "Fire!"

Joseph pulled the trigger. The adrenaline was flowing so hard through his body that he hardly felt the recoil against his shoulder, nor did he hear the rifles behind him fire. His body went through the motions of loading his rifle without thought as he kept his eyes on the enemy line. By the time the third line had fired, he was loaded and ready.

The cannons began their deadly barrage again, but the first rounds overshot the companies as they tried to get the range proper.

The colonel raised his saber. "Fix bayonets, men!"

The sergeant repeated the order as he pulled his own out and jammed it on the end of his rifle.

Joseph fixed his bayonet and stood up, the rest of his line following suit. They were still a good hundred yards from the Confederate line, and the run would be uphill, but he was young, and the blood flowed hot in his veins.

Col. "Charge!"

Joseph barely heard the command as his body lunged forward, his legs pumping faster and faster as he raced toward the Confederate soldiers. As he neared the brush, a soldier rose up and pointed his rifle. Without thinking, Joseph dodged to his left as the man fired and the bullet sang past his head. He raised his own rifle and fired, catching the man in the chest. By the time he reached the line, he was screaming like a madman and there was pounding in his ears. He leapt over the low berm the soldiers had raised and plunged his bayonet into another man. He pulled hard to free the blade and turned on his heels in time to block the thrust of another soldier. The man, off balance, fell forward. Joseph brought the butt of his rifle around and hit the man on the side of his head. The soldier dropped to the ground, motionless.

Joseph stood over the man, his breath coming in great, coughing gasps as his brain finally caught up to where he was. He looked around and saw the Confederate soldiers running as the rest of his platoon and the entire company reached the bush and charged after them.

Robert ran up and grabbed Joseph by the shoulders, his eyes wide and a grin pasted on his face. "Joseph! What happened? It was like you were possessed!"

Joseph looked around, realizing what he had done, and shook his head. "I don't know," he sputtered. "Everything seemed to slow down." He put a hand to his forehead. "I don't know what happened to me."

"I do," the sergeant said, smiling. "I've seen it before. The fever of battle gets into your blood." He looked around at the men Joseph had killed. "They didn't stand a chance."

The blood left Joseph's face, and he felt like he was going to lose his breakfast.

"Reload if you haven't already," the sergeant ordered. "We gotta get back into this fight."

Joseph reloaded his rifle and followed Robert as they advanced into the woods. A short way in they found themselves in a shallow swamp.

A couple of hundred Confederate soldiers stood around with their arms up. They had dropped their rifles at their feet at the urging of the Union soldiers.

"Well done, men!" The colonel yelled.

They had just started leading the captive soldiers out when the woods around them filled with the shrieking call of the rebel yell.

Epic Everyone froze.

The captives dove for the ground as bullets filled the air, dropping a dozen Union soldiers before they could move. Joseph grabbed Robert and ran for the tree line. Mini balls whizzed overhead, and branches splintered as they ran.

Jerome and Henry flew past them as they reached the field. As soon as they cleared the trees, they turned and dropped to one knee, bringing their rifles up to cover the trees.

Joseph and Robert joined them. More and more Union soldiers cleared the trees and continued down the slope at a run. *Joseph* "Come on!" Joseph shouted and followed at a jog. He stopped again and turned to cover the tree line. None of the Confederate soldiers were following, but the cannons began firing again, forcing them back.

Joseph continued down the slope, running toward the Union lines. A cannonball exploded behind him, and he was lifted off his feet and hurled through the air. He hit the ground hard, knocking the wind out of him. He struggled to breathe as dirt showered down on him.

Hands grabbed him and lifted him to his feet. He blinked the dirt out of his eyes and saw Henry and Robert holding him. Their mouths were moving, but the only sound Joseph could hear was a rushing noise that threatened to overwhelm him. He shook his head, but that brought unbearable pain, and he fell to his knees.

Henry and Robert dragged and carried Joseph the rest of the way to the Union lines and laid him down on the ground. Joseph opened his eyes and saw Robert's worried face hovering over him. Someone placed a hand behind his head and lifted it. A tin cup of water was brought to his lips, and he drank it in gulps.

(Cover mouth: Muffled)

"Can you hear me?" Robert yelled.

Joseph heard the words, but they were muffled and seemed to come from across a great distance. He nodded slowly, but even that small movement brought pain. He winced and put a hand to his head.

dissipate make Henry

Henry appeared and began checking Joseph for any wounds. "Looks like you got an angel on your shoulder," he said. "No holes and you still got all your limbs." Henry motioned for Robert to help. "Can you stand?"

Joseph nodded. The pain in his head was still there, but it had lessened. With his friends' help he got to his feet and leaned on his rifle. His eyes took in the field they had just crossed in their charge and retreated over. The long grass had been replaced with a sea of blue uniformed bodies. Some of the fallen soldiers were still moving, clawing their way along the ground, trying to get back. Cries filled the air.

The sergeant stood nearby, his head down. "God have mercy on them," he muttered, then turned and looked at Joseph and the others. "God have mercy on all of us. Make yourselves ready. They're ordering another charge."

The men stood as if struck dumb. Their eyes moved from the sergeant to the ruined field and back to the sergeant.

Joseph "When?" Joseph asked, breaking the silence.

"Soon," the sergeant answered. "Hoover, you've been injured. Make your way to the surgeon's tents."

Joseph could feel the others' eyes on him. "I'm fine, sergeant." He looked over at Henry. "Like he said, no holes and I got all my limbs."

"Suit yerself." the sergeant said with a shrug. "Just don't go blaming me if you get yerself killed."

The sound of bugles echoed up and down the lines, calling the men to form up.

Sarge "Load your rifles if you haven't already," he said.

Joseph loaded his rifle and moved to stand in line with his platoon. No one spoke. Even Robert remained silent as he stood next to Joseph. They exchanged glances, and Joseph could see a kind of sad acceptance in the young man's eyes.

Joseph "We'll get through this."

Robert nodded but didn't reply.

The bugles sounded again.

Sarge "Forward, march!"

The entire line surged forward to the sound of drums beating out the time of their steps. The Confederate lines remained quiet as if taunting them on. The Union cannons pounded the hilltop, finding their mark on occasion, but for the most part the shelling either fell short or did little damage when they did hit the line.

The army continued their slow march across the open space. By the time they reached the halfway point, the soldiers were stepping around the bodies lying thick on the ground. In some places they had no choice but to tread on the dead to keep from breaking formation.

As the front of the line moved forward, the Confederate cannons came to life. Joseph ducked as the sky above them filled with explosions and shrapnel. Whole sections of men caught directly under the air bursts folded in mid-step to join their comrades on the ground.

Joseph stepped forward but stopped when he felt a hand on his leg. He looked down and saw a young man lying on his back. His eyes were wide, and the whites almost glowed against his charred cheeks and forehead. Joseph knelt down next to him and gently took his hand. The soldier's mouth moved, and Joseph leaned closer.

The man's voice, almost inaudible, still hit Joseph hard. "Go back," he rasped. "You'll die."

Joseph gently laid the dying man's hand on his chest. He had no words to comfort him, so he stood up and continued on.

Three hundred yards from the Confederate's line, the rifles opened up. The concentrated fire hit the front of the army like a wall of solid lead, and the entire front of the attack dissolved.

The men in the next ranks dropped to a kneeling position and returned fire, but the Confederate soldiers were shooting from behind berms and stone walls. Only a few fell.

Another round of rifle fire shredded the companies, with whole platoons falling.

Joseph raised his rifle and fired, unsure if he hit anything. He stopped and reloaded his rifle before continuing up the slope.

The bugles sounded again. The army slowed, hesitated, and then stopped its advance. When they sounded again, the army turned and retreated toward the Rappahannock.

Joseph reached the Union lines and looked around for his friends. He found Robert leaning against a large boulder, breathing hard. "Are you hurt?"

Robert shook his head. "They beat us, Joseph. They beat us, but good."

"I know it." Joseph looked around for Jerome, Henry, and Mort.

"I haven't seen 'em," Robert coughed.

Joseph glanced up the line and saw Henry and Jerome heading toward them. Jerome had his hand on Henry's shoulder, and Henry seemed to be cradling something in his arms. As they neared, Joseph could see the glint of brass and realized that Henry carried his brother's bugle.

Henry held out the bugle. It had been twisted and smashed, and several holes were torn into the metal.

Jerome "One of the drummers brought it to him," Jerome said, still gripping Henry's shoulder. "He wanted to go back into the field to look for him."

Henry tore himself free of Jerome and walked away. He headed back to the river with the other soldiers, still cradling the bugle.

Jerom "What do we do?" Jerome asked.

Joseph watched Henry for a moment, then said, "We get back across the river before they decide to launch a counterattack."

Robert looked out over the field filled with thousands of dead and dying soldiers. "Why, Joseph? Why'd we do it?"

"Orders is orders," Joseph answered. "And we follow orders." He shouldered his rifle and headed down to the river.

Joseph stood in the field, his eyes taking in the horror around him. After returning across the Rappahannock, he had gone in search of his friend Jacob.

An hour of searching left Joseph with two thoughts: either Jacob was lying dead or dying on the battlefield, or he was lying somewhere in the area they had sectioned off for the field hospital.

Joseph had wandered in and out of some of the tents used for surgery, but the sight of doctors sawing off limbs and the screams of the men were too much, and he decided to look in the fields.

They were almost as bad.

Everywhere Joseph turned, a sea of bodies writhed or lay motionless on the ground. The sound of moaning and cries of pain struck his heart, and his eyes filled with tears. He looked down at his feet and saw a young man lying on his back, staring up at him. Joseph knelt down and offered the man water from his canteen.

The man accepted the water gratefully. Joseph moved on to another man, and then another, until his canteen was empty. He stood up and looked around to see if there were water barrels nearby to refill his canteen.

Joseph saw some barrels lined up near a tree, and he wound his way among the wounded until he reached them. He pushed his canteen under the water until it was full.

Jacob "Joseph?"

Joseph turned at the sound of his name and saw Jacob, lying in the shade of a tree, his hand covering his bloodied stomach. The sight wrenched at Joseph's heart. He lifted the canteen out of the water and rushed to his friend's side.

Joseph "I was wonderin' where you was holed up," he said, kneeling next to Jacob. He gently raised the man's head and gave him water. "Looks like you picked a good spot. Plenty of shade."

Jacob smiled. "Took me most of the day to find it," he coughed.

Joseph glanced down at the wound. Blood was slowly seeping between Jacob's fingers. His torn shirt was soaked and had started to turn black. "Have the surgeons looked at you?"

Jacob nodded. "That was 'bout all they did. Looked at me and told the guys carrying me to take me someplace nice."

He coughed again and Joseph saw that his lips were now red with blood.

Joseph "That bad?"

Jacob "Reckon so," Jacob answered. "Don't rightly know how much longer."

Joseph sat down on the ground. "I'll stay with you."

"'Preciate that."

"Are you in pain?"

Jacob shook his head. "Someone came round a while ago. Gave me some medicine. Called it morphine." He looked up at the sky. "Do you reckon I'll see 'em? The wife and boy?"

Joseph "Yeah, I reckon," Joseph answered. "Is there anything I can do for you?"

Jacob "You're doin' it." Jacob closed his eyes for a while. When he opened them, he seemed to Joseph to be far away. "How did we do? Did we win?"

Joseph "Yeah, Jacob. It will soon be over, and we can all go home."

Jacob smiled. "I hope you get to eat your mom's pickles soon."

"Me too."

Jacob took a final shallow, shuddering breath and lay still.

Joseph sat there beside his friend until the sun had set. Then he took out his pencil and found a flat piece of wood to write his friend's name. He folded Jacob's arms across his chest and laid the wood on top. Joseph took one long, last look at the man he had befriended so many months ago, then rose to his feet and headed back to where the army was camped, to hopefully find Robert and the others.

Robert watched an exhausted Joseph approach the fire. He shifted along the log he was sitting on to make room for his friend. "Thought maybe you had deserted," he said.

Joseph sat down heavily. "No," he answered. "Not before you."

Robert smiled and pulled the iron pot away from the fire. "Kept some supper for you." He spooned out what was left in the bottom of the pot and handed the cup and a spoon to Joseph.

Joseph took them gratefully. He shoved a spoonful of the stew into his mouth and chewed in silence.

"Did you find Jacob?"

Joseph lowered his head and swallowed. "Yeah. I found him."

Robert sighed. "Henry's gone off someplace."

"Mort?"

"Yeah, I think so. Jerome tried to stop him. Henry bloodied his lip."

Joseph winced at the news. "Jerome okay?"

Robert nodded. "He was spittin' mad at first, but he calmed down."

"Where is Jerome?"

"He went after Henry. Not to fight. He was worried that Henry might do somethin' stupid, like go to the other side of the river to look for Mort." Robert handed Joseph a tin of coffee. "I don't reckon he'll stop Henry from goin'. He'll just follow to keep him safe." Robert shook his head. "Been a day."

Joseph put the stew cup on the ground and took a sip of coffee. "It's been a day; no question 'bout it."

"I'm sorry about Jacob," Robert said quietly. "But I'm glad you found him."

There was silence for a bit; then Robert spoke up again. "I reckon we'll all end up dead before this is over."

"I don't know," Joseph said into his cup. "The chances might look a bit glum . . . but fussin' over it isn't going to change things. Either we live or we die. God makes that decision. Not you and not me. Not even the Rebels shootin' at us."

The two friends sat staring at the fire long into the night, each keeping to his own thoughts, and waiting for Henry and Jerome to find their way back.

SATURDAY, MAY 2, 1863

EVE OF SECOND BATTLE OF
FREDERICKSBURG, MARYE'S HEIGHTS

The young soldier ran up to the platoon as fast as he could. He skidded to a halt just short of running Joseph down and stood in front of the men, gasping for breath.

"Any word as to where we're marching?" Joseph asked. He waited patiently while the young man caught his breath.

"Speak up, boy!" Henry grunted. "We don't have all day."

"You ain't gonna like it," the young man finally got out.

"Where?"

"We's heading back to Fredericksburg."

"Oh, sweet Lord," Jerome breathed.

"What are we gonna do, Joseph?" Robert asked. His face had

gone ashen and his voice trembled a bit.

"Do?" Henry cut in. "We're gonna get even is what we're gonna do!"

Joseph looked at Henry and was shocked to see the look in his eyes. He shook his head at what the other man was thinking.

"Joseph?" Robert asked again.

"We're soldiers," Joseph answered. "We do what they tell us to do; we go where they tell us to go, and we don't question or whine about it." He turned on Henry and stood face-to-face with him. "And we don't go doin' stupid things that get the others killed." He held Henry's eyes, waiting for a response.

Henry's back stiffened and his jaw clenched, but he eventually gave Joseph a nod.

"Then we march when the higher-ups figure out when." Addressing the young man who'd brought the news, he said, "Did they say when?"

"Soon," the young man answered. "I should get back."

"Go," Joseph said. "And thank you." He got back in line with the others. "If my reckoning is right, we should be only a day's march from the Rappahannock."

"Meanin' we'll probably be in battle tomorrow," Henry said. He smiled grimly. "None too soon, if'n you ask me."

"No one's askin'," Joseph said. "Remember what I said, Henry."

"I'll remember, Joseph."

SUNDAY, MAY 3, 1863

SECOND BATTLE OF FREDERICKSBURG, MARYE'S HEIGHTS

Joseph stood in formation and stared at the town that blocked their path. They had marched all day yesterday and crossed the Rappahannock on pontoons before the sun had risen this morning. He shook his head at the thought of reliving the same horror they had encountered four months before.

The sergeant strode up and addressed the men. "We will hold this position for now," he told them. "We are acting as a diversion of sorts for the main army."

"How long do we stay here?" Henry asked.

"As long as it takes," the sergeant growled back. "If that means we stay here till the snow flies, then we stay here till the snow flies."

76

A runner came loping up the shoreline and stopped in front of the sergeant.

"Report," the sergeant ordered.

"Colonel says you are to move around the town and form up in front of a hill on the other side. You'll be joined by the rest of the Sixth."

"Well, men," the sergeant said, "looks like we won't be standing around wasting air." He moved to the front of the platoon. "Platoon, left face! Forward, march!"

Joseph began marching along the bank of the river. Robert as always, stepped in line to his right. The platoon had been diminished by death and disease, but they still formed a strong presence as they rounded the last building of the city and moved out into the open field. Joseph felt a twinge in his stomach as he caught sight of the same hill line that had cost them so much before. For a moment he thought of Jacob, and he felt the heat rise in his face. He understood Henry's urgent need to reap revenge for those who had fallen.

The sergeant led the men to a staging area where other platoons were forming up. Joseph kept an eye on the plateau as they positioned behind another platoon. He could see the Confederate soldiers moving along the lines and the barrels of their rifles. The entire line bristled with muskets, all tipped with bayonets.

"I can't believe we're doing this again," Robert whispered.

"That makes several thousand of us." Joseph looked down the line. The sight still impressed him, but he knew that looking impressive and dying unimpressively went hand in hand.

The bugles sounded up and down the line. The drummers rapped the beat that would urge them toward the enemy's lines.

Sarge "Forward, march!"

The line moved across the field toward the hill. The Confederate batteries began firing, and soon the Union formations were being hit.

The bugles sounded the charge.

Everyone started running up the slope. The maneuver helped pull the front lines out of the cannon fire, but a sudden volley of shot from Confederate rifles soon followed. The charge stalled, moved forward, and stalled again.

Joseph's platoon reached the sunken road and stone wall that ran around the base of the hill, and they squatted down behind it for protection.

Robert "This is turning out as bad as before." Robert fumbled with a cartridge as he fought to load his rifle as fast as possible.

Joseph raised his own rifle and fired. He ducked behind the stones as mini balls ripped into the stone in answer. "I reckon it is," he said as he reloaded.

The bugles sounded the retreat.

Robert "Think it's over, Joseph?"

Joseph hefted his rifle and crouched. "I think it's just started." He risked a quick glance over the wall, ducking just as more bullets ricocheted off the stone. "Now!" he screamed.

Joseph and Robert sprinted back across the field to the safety of their own lines. Henry and Jerome had already returned and were waiting for them.

Joseph turned back and saw the carnage left by the charge. Union soldiers lay scattered throughout the field, twisted in the throes of death or crawling about, trying to find shelter from the continued gunfire.

The bugles sounded again.

"Form up!" the sergeant bellowed, leaving no time for the horrific scene to unnerve his men. "Charge!"

Joseph gripped his rifle and began the run back up the hill. They stopped halfway and fired their Enfields, pausing only long enough to reload. Even that short pause cost them dearly as the combined firepower of the cannons and muskets cut into their ranks. Soldiers were falling all around Joseph and Robert, and they were showered with dirt from the explosions.

They continued up the slope and reached the road and wall a second time. The intensity of the fire doubled and tripled, cutting down whole platoons in mid-step.

The bugles sounded the retreat, and the Union charge fell apart as the men turned and ran back down the hill.

Joseph stopped as he neared the town and bent over, spilling his stomach into the dirt. Around him, others were doing the same. He wondered how many times he could charge up the hill before a musket or cannon found him and ended the torment.

The general strode out from the ranks and surveyed the battlefield. He waved a colonel to his side and they talked for a minute. A couple of mounted sergeants led the officer's horses forward. The general and the colonel mounted, and a white flag was produced.

"What do you think they're doin', Joseph?" Jerome asked.

"Maybe they're gonna ask them Rebels to surrender," Robert said.

Joseph just shook his head as he watched the small group approach the lines.

The Union officers reached the summit and the Confederate lines and spoke with officers from the other side. The groups saluted and the meeting was over. The general and others returned at a canter.

After a brief discussion with the Union officers, a lieutenant came running over and addressed the men. "We have brokered a truce with the Rebs. They will allow us to enter the battlefield and retrieve our wounded. Sergeant, have the men shoulder their arms and proceed to give succor to our fallen comrades."

The sergeant saluted the lieutenant. "Yes sir." He turned to the platoon. "Let's bring them back."

Joseph shouldered his rifle and walked onto the field with thousands of other soldiers. They worked quickly, but some of the injuries were such that it took several men to carry one wounded soldier back to where the surgeons had set up their tents. The buglers and drummers, normally used to help with the injured, now found themselves giving directions to private and officer alike.

It took almost two hours to remove the wounded to a place of safety. Joseph noticed that the general rode his horse around the battlefield, stopping every now and then to look at the Confederate lines. When they had done as much as they could for the wounded, the companies were re-formed to continue the attack.

The sergeant stood off and was speaking with several officers in what looked to Joseph like a heated exchange. The sergeant saluted and returned to the platoon. Joseph could see that he was having difficulty with what he had just been told.

"What's the news, Sarge?" Joseph asked.

The sergeant scratched his beard as he looked the men up and down. "I reckon you all know we'll be charging the lines again."

"We expected as much." Joseph said.

"Yeah," the sergeant continued. "The general was looking over the enemy lines while we was bringing the wounded back. He says they suffered heavy losses during our attacks, and the lines are spread real thin."

"That's good," Joseph said. "So why do you look like you're gonna spit in our coffee?"

The sergeant sighed heavily. "I guess there ain't no easy way to say this. The general wants a bayonet charge. He says he wants the rifles unloaded during the charge."

There was stunned silence among the men.

"Is he mad?" Henry spat.

"That'll be enough of that!" the sergeant snapped. "I grant it's askin' a lot, but if you think it through, it might work."

"Why, Sergeant?" Joseph asked.

"We run," the sergeant answered. "We run up that hill as fast as we can. Like the devil hisself was chasing behind. No stopping to shoot; no stopping to reload."

There was grumbling from the men. Joseph could see the men in the other platoons were having the same difficulty with the news. He looked back up the hill at the line. "He's right," he said quietly.

"Have you lost your senses?" Henry asked him.

"Think about it," Joseph answered. "They'll have maybe one reload before we hit their lines."

The sergeant nodded. "We'll march out in formation. When you hear the bugle call, run. Spread out; make 'em have to take time to aim. And run. Run for yer mothers and yer country."

The bugles sounded.

"Form up, men!" the sergeant called out. "Forward, march!"

Joseph stepped in line with the rest of the men, his rifle held low and ready. He had to rein himself in several times during the march to keep from breaking into a run too early. He could feel the same tension from Robert. "Steady," he said.

The bugles sounded again.

"Now, men!" the sergeant yelled.

Joseph screamed at the top of his lungs. He pushed his body forward and willed his legs to move faster and faster.

The whole front of the charge surged forward and spread out as the wave of Union soldiers hurtled steadily up the slope.

The Confederate army finally gave answer to the charge, and muskets and cannons fired in earnest at the advancing forces.

Union soldiers began dropping, but Joseph could see that fewer fell than in previous charges. He was now close enough to see the faces of the enemy soldiers and the panic in their eyes as they scrambled to reload their muskets. Even the cannon fire became sporadic and off target as the gunners fought to change the elevation fast enough to keep up with the advance.

The Confederate soldiers managed to get off one more poorly aimed round before they were overwhelmed.

Joseph's heart pounded as he forced his legs to keep moving despite the ache. He was within feet of the wall when he saw the soldiers hiding behind it rise to their feet, turn, and run.

A shout went up from the Union lines, and Joseph joined in as he leapt over the wall and chased after the fleeing soldiers. He glanced to his right and saw Robert keeping pace, his face split as he laughed and yelled at the same time.

Joseph stopped when he reached the far slope and looked down at the Confederates, their lines broken and scattered as they raced off the plateau. A shout went up from the Union army as soldiers planted the Stars and Stripes.

"We did it, Joseph!" Robert clapped him on the back.

Joseph grinned back. "Guess the general knew what he was doin' after all."

"Reckon so." Robert jutted his chin in the direction of the general and several officers who had gathered around. "Looks like they're fixing to—"

Robert was cut off by the sounding of the bugles to form ranks.

Joseph exchanged glances with Robert, Henry, and Jerome as they moved to make formation. "Do we keep advancing?" Joseph asked.

The sergeant came trotting up. "That's exactly what we're doin.' The general hopes to join up with General Hooker's forces. Together we can push the Rebs clear out of here." He gave the men a long look. "Ya did fine, men. A proud moment for the Onesers." He moved to stand a few paces ahead of the platoon. "Platoon, march!"

"What do you think they're gonna do, Joseph?" Henry asked.

They had marched along the Plank Road from the summit of Marye's Heights eastward toward a place known as Salem Church. At first the march had moved at a good pace, but several times they were hit by small bands of Rebels moving parallel to their lines. It was midafternoon before they had reached the main body of the Confederates. The Rebels had regrouped beyond the church, and the general ordered an immediate charge.

The charge had failed, and General Sedgwick was forced to pull the men back to the rim of a hill on the east side of the church.

Joseph and the other soldiers had quickly dug in and raised

a low protective berm to make their stand and were now sitting in the shallow ditch they had dug, watching the Confederate soldiers a half mile away. Joseph realized that this was one of the few times they had been dug in and the enemy would have to charge their positions. The image of Fredericksburg welled up in his mind, followed by his last conversation with Jacob. For some strange reason his mouth began to water and he thought about pickles.

"What do you think they're gonna do, Joseph?" Henry asked a second time.

Joseph cleared his thoughts and looked over the wall again. "I reckon they're gonna charge at some point." He looked back and saw the rows of their own cannons that had been brought up from the banks of the river. "They will pay a hefty price for the rights to this hill."

Henry grunted his agreement.

"Maybe we should play 'em a game of baseball!" Robert laughed. "That field yonder would be perfect for it."

Joseph smiled. "It would." Then his smile grew as he remembered the last game he'd watched in the camp. It had degenerated into a huge brawl between companies. "If'n it turned out like the last one, we'd just end up fightin' 'em anyway."

Everyone within earshot laughed.

Joseph caught movement out of the corner of his eye and stood up to get a better look. Several of the sleek Parrott cannons were being moved up to the line, along with wooden crates of bagged gunpowder and grapeshot charges.

"That's gonna tear 'em apart," Joseph muttered.

"No different than what happened to us, Joseph." Henry was looking at the cannons with a dark look in his eyes and a crooked grin on his lips. "Remember Fredericksburg? Mud run? And not more than three days ago at the crossing?" Henry spat on the ground. "They tore Mort apart."

"I remember, Henry," Joseph answered quietly. "Don't mean I can't feel sorry for 'em."

Henry "I don't. Can't. Won't."

Joseph stared at Henry. There was something in the other man's voice that sent a chill down his spine.

"We all miss Mort," Robert said. He glanced nervously at Joseph.

Joseph shrugged. He didn't know what to say or do. Henry had every right to feel the way he did.

Henry stood staring at the Confederates massing at the other end of the valley. He spat over the wall and moved to sit in the trench away from the others.

"Has he gone mad, Joseph?" Robert whispered.

"I don't rightly know," Joseph answered. "He's grievin' awful hard; I know that." Joseph closed his eyes and rested his head against the cool dirt of the berm. "Can you tell me it'd be any different for you? If'n it was your brother that got cut down?" He shook his head. "I got eleven brothers and sisters back home. One brother who'll be of the age to enlist come next year." Joseph opened his eyes and looked over at Henry with pity. "There, but for the grace of God, go I," he whispered.

"What's that?" Robert asked.

"Somethin' the preacher back home said during a sermon. It means that could be me or you sitting over yonder with an empty heart." Joseph sat up and looked over the dirt into the valley. "If Henry lives through this madness, he still has to go home."

The faint sounds of bugles drifted up from the valley. They

could see the Confederate lines tighten up.

"They're gettin' ready," Joseph called out. "Make sure you're all loaded."

An officer rode up and down the line on a black stallion, the long feather in his hat whipping in the breeze. "Hold the line, men!" he called out as he rode along. "Hold the line!"

Joseph swung his body around, cradling his rifle on his forearms, and watched as the army below began a slow march toward them. The sergeant stood behind them. "Hold your fire until I give the order," he told them.

Joseph pulled the hammer to the half cock position and sighted down the barrel. He fought to control his breathing as he waited.

The Union cannons began firing canister rounds on the advancing troops, and the effects were horrific. The grapeshot tore through the advancing soldiers with such ferocity that even the Union soldiers were shocked.

Despite the carnage the Confederates pressed the attack and were soon in range of the Enfields.

Joseph pulled the hammer to full cock and waited. He picked out a soldier and followed him with the end of the barrel.

"Fire!"

Joseph pulled the trigger and watched the soldier clutch his left shoulder before dropping to the ground. He pulled back from the berm and reloaded, returned to his position, found another target, and waited.

"Fire!"

Again, Joseph pulled the trigger and another soldier lay dead or dying. He squinted through the smoke and saw that the advance had stalled. Joseph reloaded and waited.

"Men, fire at your convenience!"

Joseph searched the confusion of the battlefield and saw the soldier holding the Confederate colors. He aimed and pulled the trigger. The colors fell, still clutched in soldier's hands.

Joseph watched as another Confederate ran toward the flag and lifted it high. A shot from another Union soldier somewhere along the line took the man in the chest, and he fell to his knees. Another Confederate took hold of the flag's staff before it could fall. The soldier cried out as he was hit by multiple rounds. He slumped over, but somehow managed to keep the flag from falling to the ground.

Joseph watched as more Confederate soldiers ran to rescue their flag. He knew what would happen. An army's flag was both the center of honor and a means to communicate commands, and to let it fall was a mark of defeat. He had watched Union soldiers die by the handful keeping the Stars and Stripes flying on the battlefield.

The firing continued, and the whole front of the Confederate charge became rows of dead and dying. More bugles sounded, and the Rebels retreated back into the valley. The cannons and rifle fire died, and the enemy was able to drag and carry their wounded back to the safety of their original lines.

Joseph sighed in relief and sat back down. He wiped the sweat from his forehead and laid his rifle across his knees.

"They took it hard," Robert said. He sat down and put his head in his hands.

"They'll be back for more." Jerome stood and reloaded his rifle.

"Seems like a waste, if you ask me." Robert's voice was thick and raspy. "They should just leave."

"For the same reason we didn't leave when we took that last hill," Joseph answered. "It's war. Armies gotta fight in wars."

"Then we should be chasin 'em now," Henry said. He raised his rifle and took aim.

Joseph stood and took a quick look at what Henry was aiming at. All he could see were some Confederate soldiers carrying wounded. "You put that musket down, Henry Timnerman."

Henry looked at Joseph. "I'm a corporal. I don't take orders from a private." He spat on the ground.

"Then you'll take 'em from me!" The sergeant had walked up and stood behind Henry. "Pull that trigger and I'll stove in the back of your head."

Henry lowered his rifle. "They're the enemy," he said.

"They's enemies when they're a-chargin. They's enemies when they's shootin' at us and they's enemies when we are chargin'." The sergeant moved to stand in front of Henry. "But right now, they's just men trying to help their fellow men."

Henry stood silent, but his face was a storm cloud of anger. He spat over the wall, turned on his heels, and headed down the trench.

Joseph stood next to the sergeant, watching Henry stump away. "Thanks, Sarge. I was thinking I might have to stop him."

"He's not right, is he? I mean, right in the head."

Joseph kicked at the dirt. "Mort dyin' the first time we was here lays heavy on him." He watched as Henry found a spot farther down the trench and sat down, burying his face in his hands. "It's like he's lookin' to get himself killed."

"I seen it before," the sergeant said. "Like as not, I'll see it again many times before I get to go home or go to an early grave."

"I'll keep an eye on him."

"You do that." The sergeant jutted his chin toward the valley. "Best get yourselves ready. Looks like they're gettin' ready to come at us again."

Joseph headed back to his spot on the line and knelt down next to Robert. The Union cannons began firing again as the Confederate officers led another charge up the hill.

Short Robert "Henry goin' to be okay?" Robert shouted over the noise. He craned his neck to see Henry farther down the line.

"I don't rightly know!" Joseph shouted back. He gave Robert a nudge with his elbow. "Best watch in front! Henry can take care on his own!" Joseph aimed his rifle down the hill and pulled the hammer back. He found his chosen mark and pulled the trigger.

Joseph sat by the fire, sipping strong coffee from his cup. He had left the line shortly after the sun had gone down, and the sergeant had told the men that there would be no more action until morning. Joseph's platoon drew second watch, and he still had a few hours before he would have to return to the wall.

A noise made him sit up, and he watched as Henry walked out of the darkness and sat down next to Joseph at the fire.

Joseph found another cup and filled it with the hot brew. He held it out to Henry without saying anything.

Henry looked at the cup for a moment before finally accepting it with a curt nod.

The two sat staring into the fire in silence. Joseph glanced at Henry from time to time, trying to gauge his thoughts. "Everything quiet on the line?" he asked, breaking the heavy silence.

Henry nodded.

Joseph finished his coffee and placed his cup on the ground.

"Where are the others?" Henry asked.

"Sleeping," Joseph answered. "We're to take up the watch at the second hour." Joseph cleared his throat. "Might be best if you got some sleep yerself. Been quite the day."

Henry spat into the fire. "Would you really have stopped me?"

Joseph stretched his legs out beside the fire. "I reckon I would have tried."

"Why?"

"Why?" Joseph repeated. "You think Mort would have let you shoot those men? You think Mort isn't lookin' down at us right now? At you? I tell you he *is* lookin', and he sees you." Joseph tried to keep the anger out of his voice, but he could feel it building. He cleared his throat and closed his mouth.

"I know it." Henry took a sip of his coffee.

"I know you're sad and angry about Mort gettin' killed." Joseph spoke quietly and with more control over his voice. "We all are. I know Mort wasn't blood with us, but you don't need to have the same blood flowing through yer veins to be family." He waved his hand at the tents where Jerome and Robert were sleeping. "We've come to be brothers. All that we've been through, how can we not?"

"I reckon." Henry drained his cup. "Any more?" he asked, holding his cup toward Joseph.

Joseph grabbed the pot out of the fire and refilled Henry's cup. He picked up his own and filled it before setting the pot next to the fire.

"Since the start I been trying to figure out why we all ended up together. Why us?"

Hen "Like long-lost brothers," Henry commented dryly.

Jos "Poke fun if you want." Joseph looked up at the stars. "Somethin' brought us together so we'd watch out for each other. Same as brothers would."

Henry "That kinda thinkin' is beyond me," Henry said.

Joseph "Well, we all thought you was the slow one in the family." Joseph smiled kindly at Henry.

Henry tried to smile, but tears suddenly began sliding down his face. He raised a hand and wiped them away. "First time I cried since Mort . . ." His voice got thick and he stopped talking.

"No sin to cry," Joseph said quietly. Silence returned, and the two men sat staring into the flames or up at the night sky.

"Why are you here, Joseph?"

"Not sure what you mean."

"Why'd you sign up?"

Joseph rubbed his beard. "Not sure I know, leastways not for certain."

"Doesn't sound like somethin' you'd say." Henry looked at Joseph. "I always took you fer knowing things the rest of us didn't."

"Well, I signed up because it seemed like the thing to do. All the young men in the county were puttin' their names on the rolls." Joseph turned so he could see Henry. "I come from a big family. The money from soldierin' would help them."

"That's a good reason, as reasons go." Henry spat in the fire.

"It was."

"Was?" Henry asked. "You have a change of heart?" He shook his head. "You're no deserter, Joseph. If'n you were, you'd have gone a long time ago."

"That's not what I mean," Joseph said. "I still think signin' my name to send money home was a good idea. But it's not what makes me fight. Not anymore."

"Freein' the slaves?"

Joseph shrugged. "I reckon it's a noble enough idea."

"And the Rebs? They fightin' to keep the slaves."

"You think most of 'em have slaves?" Joseph asked. "The officers come from big, rich families. I reckon they'd own slaves, but the soldiers? The privates, corporals, and sergeants? They're as poor as you and me. I can't afford a slave, nor would I want one."

"Me neither," Henry said, shaking his head. "So what do you think they're fightin' for?"

"Dunno. I'll ask next time I talk to one."

Henry laughed.

"So why did you sign up?" Joseph asked.

Henry's face became serious. "Mort wanted to join up. He was eighteen, so we couldn't stop him." Henry gripped his cup tight in both hands. "I promised our mom I'd look out for him. Keep him safe." Tears formed in his eyes again. "I don't know what I'm gonna say to her if I make it home."

"I'm sorry."

"Yeah. Me too."

Joseph wasn't sure what to do or say next. "Why did Mort want to join?" he finally asked.

Henry frowned at the memory. "He was young. Going to war seemed the right thing to do."

"He was a good man."

"There was a Negro family in our town. He was the black-smith's helper. He had a wife and boy. The boy was the same age as Mort. They got to be friends." Henry took a sip of his now cold coffee and grimaced. "This stuff really is bad," he said.

Joseph grabbed the pot and refilled Henry's cup.

"Some Southerners came to town on business. They got to drinkin' and saw the smith's helper walkin' home. They followed. When they got to their home just outside of town, they decided to have some fun. It got ugly. They shot the father and his son. What they did to her was worse. The shots brought the neighbors runnin'. The men were still there, but they had guns. They got on their horses and headed south. The woman died a couple of days later."

"And Mort?"

"It was hard for him. He couldn't understand why people would do that." Henry took a deep breath and let it out as a sigh. "War broke out, and he wanted to join right away. I managed to talk him down, but after a while he wouldn't listen."

"And here we are," Joseph said quietly.

"Yeah. Here we are."

The sergeant walked into the light and sat down. He looked at Joseph and then looked long and hard at Henry. "You get your senses back?" he asked.

"Yes sir."

"That's good." He scratched the side of his face. "Wake the others. We got orders to move north and cross back over the river."

"We retreatin'?" Joseph asked in surprise. "I thought we were winnin' this one."

The sergeant got to his feet. "I don't ask questions. I follow orders. And so do you." He waved his hand at the tents. "Get them up. We leave in an hour." With that, he left to find the next camp.

Henry sat with a stunned look on his face. "So today, all of it was for nothin'."

Joseph rose to his feet. "Yeah." He headed to the tent he shared with Robert. "Wake Jerome up. It's gonna be a long march."

11

TUESDAY, MAY 3, 1864

THE OVERLAND CAMPAIGN AND ON TO WILDERNESS

Joseph stood on the banks of the river Rapidan and watched as the army engineers moved pontoon after pontoon into positions at the water's edge. The morning's mist still drifted along the river's surface, partially hiding the far bank, but he knew from the scout reports that the enemy was still at least two days' march away.

Leut "Sergeant!"

Joseph let his eyes wander as he searched for any break in the morning fog that would give him at least a momentary glimpse to ease his worry.

Levt "Sergeant Hoover!"

Joseph's head jerked around at the sound of his name. He saw the lieutenant sitting on his horse several yards away. He was only a few years older than Joseph, but he bore himself as if he had been an officer since birth. He wore a goatee, and his long, dark hair fell almost to his shoulders. The lieutenant was new to the company, but Joseph had taken a liking to him from the first day. There was no doubting the man's courage under fire, and the men respected him.

Joseph strode over and saluted. "Yes, sir! Sorry. I was lost in thought."

The lieutenant returned the salute and smiled. "No apologies necessary, Sergeant. I am always <u>awed</u> by the sight of an army preparing for battle." He pointed his goatee at Joseph's arms. "How are the stripes fitting?"

Joseph's left hand automatically went to his right shoulder and felt the still-new chevrons he had sewn on himself not a month earlier. "Still getting used to 'em, sir."

The lieutenant nodded. "It was the same for me when I graduated and got my commission. It'll wear on you soon enough."

"Yes, sir."

"Are the men ready?"

"Yes, sir, they are. Even the new replacements. I took them under my wing, so to speak. They'll give whatever you ask of them."

"Good. Very good, Sergeant. It's <u>partly</u> due to the reputation you Onesers <u>have</u> that I asked for this regiment."

"We won't let you down, sir."

"I know it well, Sergeant. I'll let you get back to your men. We'll meet later at my tent for briefing on tomorrow's maneuvers."

Joseph nodded and snapped a salute at the lieutenant. He watched as the man galloped away, then turned his attention back to the river. The mist still clung stubbornly to the water, and Joseph gave up trying to see through it. He turned away and headed back to camp.

Joseph found Robert sitting by the fire, stirring the same cast iron pot they had all bought during their second week of training. With his newly minted stripes, Joseph was able to acquire a small cast iron pan, which became invaluable for meals. He saw Robert putting strips of salted bacon onto the pan and resting it on the fire.

"Don't be burning the bacon," Joseph warned.

Robert looked up with a grin. "Was wondering where you had gone off to. Thought maybe you'd deserted."

Joseph grinned and sat down. "Not before you."

Jerome stuck his head out of the tent and burped. "Smells good," he said. He gave his foot a kick, and they heard Henry yell out. "Get yer lazy self up." Jerome climbed out of the tent followed close behind by Henry.

Joseph looked at Henry and noticed the man appeared as if he'd just gone to bed. His hair had taken on a wild look over the last few months, but now it looked like more like a nest for possums. "How much did you lose last night?" Joseph asked.

Henry sat down hard and scratched his head. "Don't remember. Someone brought a jug. Things got a bit blurry after the cork was lost."

"Hmm," Joseph mumbled. "At least I'm not pulling you out of the stockade."

"There is that." Henry spat on the ground next to him. "Coffee ready?"

Robert gave the pot one last stir. "It's a bit strong"—he glanced at Henry—"but I'm thinkin' that's not a bad thing today."

Everyone held out their tin cups while Robert poured the hot liquid. The aroma filled the air around them, and there was a chorus of sighs as they sipped.

"Nothin' wrong with strong," Jerome said.

"How's the bacon comin'?" Joseph asked.

"Be ready soon enough. Got some bread last night on a trade. I'll cut slices and toast 'em." Robert took out a small bundle wrapped in cloth and opened it up. He held the loaf up to his nose. "It's only a couple of days old."

Robert finished preparing breakfast, and the small group ate in silence.

"Any idea when we leave?" Henry asked after cleaning his plate with a chunk of bread and tossing it on the ground.

Joseph looked at the filthy mess of a man sitting next to him and wrinkled up his nose. "We'll form up before first light tomorrow." He finished his coffee and looked at Robert and Jerome. "You boys have what we need?"

They set their plates aside and nodded.

"Good," Joseph said. He put his cup down. "Now!"

The three men leapt to their feet and charged Henry. Henry looked up just in time to see the others pile on top of him. There was a brief minute of wrestling and yelling before they managed to get Henry's flailing arms and legs under control. They lifted him up and started carrying him to the river.

"What are youse doin'?" Henry growled. "Have youse lost what little wits you have?"

"You stink, Henry!" Joseph yelled back. "It's gettin' so we can't sit near you!"

"And I have to share a tent with you!" Jerome added.

They reached the river's edge and stopped. "You got the shears?" Joseph asked.

Robert produced a huge pair of scissors and grinned. "Got 'em right here, Sergeant!"

"Start cutting!"

Henry started squirming even harder, tossing his head from side to side. Robert got a good fistful of the greasy locks and started cutting. "Best not fuss so much, Henry," he advised. "I might lop off an ear."

That calmed Henry down, and he stopped moving, but he continued to glare at them as Robert cut off handfuls of hair.

"It's done," Robert said, cutting off the last bit off the top. He took a look at his handiwork. "He still stinks though."

"Then let's get 'im wet." Joseph and Jerome carried Henry out into the slow current and dropped him.

Henry hit the water with a splash and sank to the bottom. He surfaced sputtering and swinging his fists, looking for something to hit.

Joseph and the others quickly backed away.

Henry stopped swinging and sat down in the water, his hands wiping the water from his eyes.

Joseph pulled out a brick of lye soap and tossed it at Henry. "You don't come out until both you and your clothes are clean." He turned and strode out of the water. "Keep an eye on him. If he tries to come out before he's clean, come and get me. He can sit in the stockade till he agrees."

"Yes, Sergeant!" Jerome and Robert said in unison.

Joseph stood at the edge of their camp, his eyes scanning the army's encampment. It was a sea of tents with thousands of men moving about. Here and there, clumps of soldiers played at cards or dice. A section of the field had been cleared, and a game of baseball had started. The cleared section was ringed with soldiers sitting or standing, cheering on their friends. Joseph wondered how long it would take for a fight to break out.

A noise behind him brought him around, and he saw Henry enter the small camp, naked. He carried his wet clothes in his arms.

"You must be clean," Joseph commented. "I didn't smell you comin'." He looked at Henry's head. "Your hair looks, well, shorter."

Henry spat on the ground. "Was that necessary?"

"It was," Joseph answered. "The lieutenant caught wind of you yesterday and ordered me to clean you up."

"Oh." Henry frowned. He began spreading his clothes on the branches of a tree.

"You plannin' on staying naked the rest of the day?"

Henry threw a sour look at Joseph, then up his clothes and ducked into his tent. A short time later he emerged with clean long underwear on and a white cotton shirt and leggings in his hands.

Joseph furrowed his brow. "You've had clean clothes all this time?"

Henry sat down on an upturned log and pulled the shirt over his head. "These are Mort's."

"Oh," Joseph muttered.

Henry finished dressing. He looked down at his bare feet. "I hope my boots dry."

"Put 'em close to the fire," Joseph advised.

Henry did as Joseph suggested. "So we head out in the morning? Any idea as to where?"

"I'll find out later this afternoon. The lieutenant will brief me and the other sergeants."

"They're sayin' Grant's pushin' to move south."

"Who's sayin'?" Joseph asked. He grabbed the pot of coffee and poured out two tin cups. He handed one to Henry.

"The men from the Sixty-third. It was them I was playing cards with last night." Henry took the cup. "Thanks."

Joseph shook his head. "You know that sort of talk is dangerous," he said. "If an officer had chanced by or one of them boys decided to take a disliking to yer face."

"I know, Joseph." Henry replied. "It was them doing the talkin'. I was just listenin'." He slapped an earlobe with his finger. "Remember?"

"Yeah, you can hear a fly fart at fifty yards." Joseph took a long drink of his coffee. "I'm just surprised you can remember anythin' from last night."

Henry chuckled. "It was before the jug appeared."

Joseph looked at Henry's bare feet. The soles were covered in blisters. "Where are your socks?"

Henry looked at his feet. "Rotted off, I reckon. Don't rightly know when."

"I'll check with the quartermaster today. See if I can get you a pair."

"Why you doin' this?"

"What do you mean?"

"Why you doin' all this for me? For Robert and Jerome?" He tossed the rest of his coffee away. "When they made you up to sergeant, they moved you to C Company. You could have just gone and not be bothered with us. At least not with me. I can understand Robert and even Jerome. They don't give you the trouble I bring."

"You're not that much trouble," Joseph said quietly. "Besides, I told you we were family." He got to his feet. "I'll be back later." He pointed at Henry's feet. "Best stay off those till I get back."

Joseph left the camp and headed toward the area that housed the headquarters, hospital tents, and the quartermaster.

It was late in the afternoon when he finally made it back to his tent. Robert, Jerome, and Henry were sitting around the fire, drinking coffee. He noticed that Henry was still barefoot. He reached into his haversack and pulled out a small jar with a cork stopper. "Here," he said tossing the jar at Henry.

"What is it?"

"It's for yer feet. Doc says to spread it on the soles and then put yer socks on." Joseph reached into his sack again and pulled out a pair of gray wool socks. He tossed those to Henry too and sat down. "Keep doing that every night before you bed down."

"Thanks." Henry pulled out the cork and took a sniff. "Ugh! What's it made from?"

Joseph shook his head. "Don't know. Doc says it's good and potent, so do as you're told."

Robert and Jerome started laughing.

"What's so funny?" Henry demanded.

"We just got you smelling nice," Robert laughed.

Joseph smiled at the jest. "Any chance I can get some of that coffee?"

Robert filled a tin cup and handed it over. "Any news on what's goin' on?"

Joseph shook his head. "I'll know more after the meeting tonight." He looked at the sky. "Speaking of, I'd best get goin'." He gulped down the coffee and stood up. He gave Henry a long look. "Stay here tonight."

"Yes, Pa," Henry said. Then he smiled.

Joseph wound his way to the colonels' tents and found several of the other sergeants had already arrived. He ducked his head in greeting and found a spot out of the way to stand. Another sergeant, several years older than Joseph, walked over to stand next to him. They nodded at each other.

"Name's Edwards." the man said, holding out his hand.

Joseph took the hand and shook it. "Hoover."

"Word is we're heading south on the morrow."

"You know more than me," Joseph answered carefully. It always made him uncomfortable talking about orders and plans with others.

The other man grunted and spat on the ground before wandering off.

The main tent flap opened, and several captains and lieutenants exited. They stood in a loose semicircle, and the gathered sergeants moved to stand next to their company commanders. Joseph spotted his own lieutenant and stood next to him.

The tent flap opened again, and General Upton emerged. Joseph had seen the man several times, and each time he felt a surge of pride at serving under him. Upton wasn't much older than Joseph, but he carried himself like a man who'd seen the world and was willing and able to jump into any challenge put before him.

The general regarded the men before speaking.

"As you are aware, we are embarking on a rather ambitious

campaign with the hopes of bringing General Lee's forces to their knees. I cannot and will not get into specifics with you sergeants for reasons I am sure you can appreciate. Your commanding officers have been given their orders and will lead you with the utmost competency just as you, in turn will lead your men and garner their best efforts on the field of battle." He looked at the men, letting his words sink in. "I have total confidence in your abilities as soldiers to win the day. That is all."

The men stood to attention and saluted.

Joseph was quiet on the walk back. The lieutenant waited until they had left the area before breaking the silence.

"I know that wasn't much in the way of information, Sergeant, but you must understand we need secrecy if we are to surprise the enemy."

"I understand, sir."

"Good. Have the men ready before first light. We'll form up at the river and make the crossing. After that . . . well, after that I'll give you a bit more of what we'll be doing."

"Good 'nuff for me, sir." Joseph saluted and continued on alone to the camp, wondering what he would say.

"What took you so long?" Robert asked. He handed Joseph a cup of stew and a spoon. "Thought maybe you'd deserted."

"Not before you," Joseph answered. "We cross the river at sunrise," he said around a mouthful of food. "Best get yerselves ready before we bed down."

"Any news as to where we're headed?" Jerome asked.

"You know better than that," Joseph said. "I get about as much information as you."

Henry chuckled and spat into the fire. "We do as we're told."

"Yes, Henry," Joseph answered. "We does as we're told.

Make it an early night. We got a long march tomorrow." Joseph finished off the stew and went to his tent, leaving the others to their thoughts.

Joseph strode up and down the lines of men that made up the platoon under his command. He smiled as he passed Henry, noting that he appeared cleaner and more like a soldier than he had in months. Robert had taken his former place in rank, and Jerome had moved to stand to Robert's right. He looked over the faces of the other men. He knew their names and some information about them, but he hadn't really gotten to know them. A brief regret washed over him for that. They seemed decent people and had distinguished themselves well in the battles since Salem Church.

He reached the rear of the formation, where he had placed the new recruits. They stood ramrod straight, and it appeared as if they were about to faint. "Ease up, lads," he said under his breath. "We're not parading for a bunch of generals."

The young men visibly relaxed.

Joseph headed back to the front and waited. The sun was just beginning to lift above the eastern horizon when a bugle sounded. Joseph stiffened his posture slightly. "Forward, march!"

He led the platoon down to the water's edge. He paused long enough to speak to the men. "Leave space between you, and try not to fall in." He stepped onto the planks covering the first pontoon and moved cautiously across the river, suddenly worried that he would lose his balance and fall in—something Robert, Henry, and Jerome would never let him forget. By the time he reached the far shore, he was sweating profusely from concentrating.

He breathed a sigh of relief and stood aside as the rest of the platoon stepped onto the bank. Once everyone was across, Joseph led them to their position along the seemingly endless ranks of soldiers.

The head of the column had already begun to move south, but it still took a half hour before Joseph's platoon could move. They marched along the bank for a short distance before veering south along a cart path.

The sun continued to rise overhead, and with it the spring heat. By noon everyone was wet with sweat and covered in dust. A halt was called, and everyone left the roadway for the shade of the trees. The only food they could eat was hardtack and water. The tough biscuit stuck in their throats, and the warm water did little to quench their thirst.

"What I wouldn't give for a jug," Henry said around a mouthful of hardtack. "This stuff could choke a horse."

"You think the drink would make this stuff taste better?" Robert asked. He dropped one of the biscuits onto the ground and crushed it with the butt of his rifle.

"Like as not," Henry answered, "but after a few snorts I wouldn't care."

Everyone within earshot laughed.

Joseph came up and stood in the shade for a minute. He took his kepi off and wiped his forehead. "How are the feet doing?"

Henry held up a booted foot. "Haven't fallen off yet."

"Good." Joseph waved the other men to their feet. "We got word to move out. We are supposed to make it to a place called Wilderness Tavern by sundown."

"Where is that?" Robert asked, getting to his feet and shouldering his rifle.

"As chance would have it," Joseph said, "same place we're headin'."

Henry gave Robert a cuff on the head.

"Ow! What was that for?"

"Askin' stupid questions," Henry laughed.

The men began marching again, and Joseph asked the drummer to march alongside and give a good marching beat. They marched along at a good pace for some time, but the sheer size of the army made for bottlenecks along the roadway, and they spent most of the afternoon resting in the trees.

By five in the afternoon, Joseph knew they would never make it to their destination. He ran ahead and spoke with the lieutenant. He returned to the platoon and marched alongside Jerome and Henry. "We'll march another hour or so, then turn east. We'll be deep in this mess of trees and undergrowth they call the Wilderness, but there's nothin' for it." He cocked his head to the men. "Pass it along that we'll be making camp in about two hours."

Henry and Jerome nodded, and Joseph slowed until he was even with the new recruits. The young men looked like they were holding up fairly well under the heat. He quick marched until he was at the head of the line and counted the beats of the drum in his head while he tried to ignore the pain in his legs and back.

Joseph and the others finally made camp in the thick underbrush. They spent some time clearing an area and setting up the tents and fire pit before they settled in to making their supper. The sun had set, and the closeness of the trees and scrub made the darkness deeper than normal. It seemed to have an effect on the men. They spoke in hushed tones, and each of them would turn a head from time to time to scan the blackness that surrounded the small circle of light from the campfire.

"How close do you think the Rebs are?" Robert asked. He had gone to wash the pot out at a small creek they had crossed earlier and returned with the pot full of water to make coffee.

"Miles from here, I'd reckon. Why?" Joseph had been writing in his diary, but he paused to answer the other's question.

"Just a feelin' I got at the creek. Like we was being watched."

Henry chuckled. "'Fraid of the dark, I expect."

"Am not!" Robert shot back.

His raised voice caused Henry to startle and look around.

"See?" Robert said, this time in a quieter tone. "You're feelin' it too; otherwise, why look at the trees?"

Henry scowled.

"We're all feelin' it," Joseph said. "Robert, get the coffee going. Keep busy and you'll be less troubled. It's just the trees being so close, I reckon." He glanced around. "I would never have thought you could hide the whole Sixth Corps in a bush, but I'll be hanged if I can see the other campfires."

"Ain't right," Henry growled under his breath.

Joseph put his diary inside his coat and stood up. "No, but it's still just a forest. I'm gonna go and check on the others. Have the coffee ready for when I get back." He turned and walked in the direction he thought he had seen some of the platoon making camp before the sun had set.

Joseph had to force his way through the underbrush, and he was scratched in a dozen places before he finally found the rest of the platoon. They had chosen to camp close together, but despite their numbers, they still spoke in quiet tones, and they all had the same habit of checking the trees around them.

Joseph spent time with the men trying to bolster their spirits before pushing his way back to his own fire. He arrived exhausted from his efforts and sat down. Robert handed him a cup of coffee and sat next to him.

"Gettin' out of here won't come soon enough if you ask me," Robert whispered. "This place is . . ."

"Yeah," Joseph agreed. "The rest of the men are feeling it too. So am I." He gulped the coffee, grimacing at the bitter taste. "We'll be out of it by tomorrow. It's no good tryin' to fight a battle in all of this." He tossed the rest of his coffee. "Best get to bed, all of you."

"We settin' a watch?" Henry asked.

"The new recruits are doing the watch for this area, so get as much rest as you can." Joseph stood up. "I'll see you in the morning."

12

THURSDAY, MAY 5, 1864

BATTLE OF WILDERNESS BEGINS

Joseph knelt beside the trunk of a tree and motioned for the rest of the platoon to stop. His eyes searched the thick underbrush for any signs of movement. He had received word from the lieutenant that the enemy had been seen moving along the turnpike and up into the bush, possibly trying to outflank the Union forces.

Joseph stiffened at the sound of movement in the brush ahead. He turned and motioned for the men to hold their positions and to ready their weapons. Joseph pulled the hammer on his rifle to the full cock position and leveled the barrel at the underbrush directly in front.

The brush parted in several places as Confederate soldiers

emerged. They moved slowly in a crouch, their rifles held at the ready.

Joseph aimed and took a deep breath. "Fire!" He pulled the trigger as he gave the command, and the surrounding forest was filled with the deafening sounds of rifles firing.

Several of the Confederate soldiers fell, while the others moved to take cover behind trees. Joseph stood behind a tree and reloaded. The Rebels returned fire, and the air was filled with the sounds of mini balls striking trees and branches. Joseph heard at least two men scream out as the bullets found their mark.

"Fix bayonets!" Joseph jammed his bayonet on the end of his rifle. A quick look told him that the rest of the platoon was following his command. "Charge!" Joseph leapt out from behind the tree and ran.

The Confederate soldiers were caught trying to reload their rifles. They turned and ran back into the underbrush, with Joseph and the others close behind. Joseph fired again, and another soldier fell. He continued on, but he lost sight of the fleeing soldiers in the thick tangle of new growth.

Joseph slowed his advance and called to his platoon to hold. "Reload!" He began reloading his rifle as his eyes scanned the area in front. He could hear branches breaking and the yells and curses of Rebel soldiers as they pushed their way through. He worried that if his men continued at a blind run, they would end up crashing into an ambush.

He pulled his platoon in, and they continued forward at a cautious pace. Soon the trees began to thin and even the underbrush lessened as they moved through the forest. Joseph could see the sky up ahead and realized that they were nearing the edge of a clearing. He held up his hand to tell the others to stop.

Robert and Henry moved to his side. "What is wrong?" Robert asked.

Joseph "There's a clearing ahead," Joseph answered. He looked up and down the line. "How far are the other platoons?"

No one knew.

Joseph frowned. "I don't want to fret over somethin' that may be nothin', but—"

Henry "We got 'em on the run, Joseph," Henry interrupted. "I say we keep 'em runnin'."

Joseph took a deep breath, trying to clear his thoughts. "I don't like it. If I had my druthers, I'd wait for the rest of the company to form up." He pointed a finger at Robert. "Head over to one of the new recruits. Have them double back and find the lieutenant and give him our location."

Robert saluted and set off as quick as he could.

Henry "So we sit and wait?" Henry asked.

Joseph shook his head. "Come on; we're gonna scout ahead. Keep low."

The two men crawled forward through the underbrush until they reached the edge of the trees. Joseph saw that the forest opened up into a pocket of tall grass several hundred feet across. The trees on the other side looked just as daunting and at least a thousand feet away. The grass offered some cover, but Joseph realized that it would also provide cover for any Confederate soldiers waiting to ambush them.

He cocked his head back and followed Henry back into the trees.

Joseph "We are going to wait," Joseph said.

Henry nodded. "That field could be filled with Rebs, and

we wouldn't know it until they fired in our faces."

Joseph "Good to see you thinkin' with yer head rather than going off half-cocked."

They moved back to where the rest of the platoon was waiting. It took Robert almost a half hour before he returned. He was breathing heavy, and his face was covered in sweat.

Robert "Found the lieutenant," he panted.

Joseph "What are his orders?" Joseph asked.

Robert "Wait here. He's comin' up with the rest of the company."

Joseph "Good. If that *is* an ambush, at least we'll have enough rifles to fight back."

The lieutenant soon arrived, and the forest was suddenly full of Union soldiers. The other sergeants ordered the men to spread out along the line that Joseph's platoon had formed.

Lent "Do we know what is out there?" the lieutenant asked.

Josef "A large field with tall grass," Joseph answered. "It's a good thousand feet or so to the next tree line."

Lent "So we'll be exposed," the lieutenant said thoughtfully.

Joseph "We could split the men and move around the field, keeping just inside the tree line," Joseph suggested.

The lieutenant shook his head. "We can't split our force. Should one run into heavy resistance, it would be cut off from the other." He looked at the men on the line. "No, we'll move cautiously through the field."

Joseph "Yes, sir," Joseph said.

Up and down the line, the other sergeants passed along the command and the entire company began moving past the trees and into the sunlight.

The company had made it twenty feet into the tall grass, and Joseph began to feel as if they would make it across without any contact. The thought vanished when a rebel yell went up and at least a hundred Confederate soldiers rose up from the grass and fired. Dozens of Union soldiers fell to the ground as the attackers dropped down into the grass. Another line of Confederate soldiers rose up and fired again.

Joseph and the others dropped and returned fire. Some of the enemy soldiers fell from gunshot, but most melted into the grass.

The lieutenant ordered a retreat, and they moved back into the safety of the trees.

"We need to move back at least a hundred feet and form up," the Lieutenant said. "We'll dig trenches and cut down some trees to lay in their path. If they wish to attack us, we'll make it as difficult as we can."

Joseph nodded and waved for the men in his platoon to follow.

When they reached the point the lieutenant had suggested, they immediately went to work with shovels and the butts of their rifles. It only took a few minutes for the men to raise a three-foot earthwork that ran for at least five hundred feet. They then cut down several small trees and laid them along the path the Rebels would have to take to reach the line.

No sooner had they finished when they heard the familiar, high-pitched rebel yell. Joseph looked around at the trees. The yell seemed to come from everywhere, and it always sent a chill down his spine. But this yell wasn't the same sound coming from many voices. It was a chorus of different yells, and it echoed along the line.

"Ready!" Joseph called out. He knelt down behind the earthwork they had put up and pointed his rifle into the trees.

There was a loud crashing, and a broken wave of gray smashed through the underbrush.

"Fire!" Joseph yelled and pulled the trigger all at the same time.

The entire Union line erupted in sound and smoke.

Confederate soldiers dropped in numbers too great to count. Joseph pulled back from the line to reload as the soldiers behind moved forward. The thick growth made it impossible for the Confederates to form a unified charge, and they tripped and scrambled instead of attacking as a line.

"Fire!"

Another volley of Union fire tore the attack apart, and the Rebel soldiers turned and ran back into the trees. Joseph finished reloading and took his place back at the berm. "Be ready for another charge!" Joseph yelled up and down the line. Robert, Henry, and Jerome were not far away.

Sporadic fire from the trees sent mini balls crashing into the berm and trees around the line. Two Union soldiers fell to Joseph's right. The line prepared for another charge, but it never came. Intermittent fire continued, but the soldiers had taken cover and the rounds failed to find any human marks. Joseph crouched behind the barricade and moved along the line to find the lieutenant.

He found the officer sitting in the trench with his back to the berm. He was nursing a wound in his arm.

"How bad?" Joseph asked.

The lieutenant shook his head. "Just a graze." He looked both ways, checking on the men. "How many did we lose?"

"Two at my end, but not from the charge," Joseph answered. "I reckon they'll keep to the trees and try to pick at us for a while."

"They'll wait for reinforcements," the lieutenant growled. "That's when they'll come at us again." He lifted his body up and peered over the dirt. "We took the wind out of them this time."

"And we'll do it again," Joseph said. "Tryin' a charge in this mess is—"

"Insane," the lieutenant finished.

Joseph looked up at the treetops. There were gaps in the leaves, and he could see that the sky had darkened. "It's late afternoon, I reckon."

The lieutenant took out a pocket watch. "It's four o'clock." He smiled when he saw Joseph looking at the timepiece. "Gift from my parents when I graduated from West Point."

"I got a sewing kit." Joseph smiled back. "I reckon both have been useful in their own way."

"I reckon," the lieutenant chuckled. "I doubt they'll chance another charge this late in the day. Keep half the men at the ready. Let the others get what rest they can." He held the watch out to Joseph. "Can you read this?"

Joseph looked at the watch and nodded.

"Take it. Just a loan, mind you," the lieutenant said, placing the timepiece in Joseph's hand. "One hour after midnight, have the men change watch. I'm afraid you and the other sergeants won't get much sleep tonight."

Joseph took the watch and tucked it into his coat next to his diary. "Wasn't plannin' on getting' any sleep anyway."

Joseph moved up and down the line, passing along the lieutenant's orders before returning to his place next to Robert.

They waited in silence, watching for any signs of an attack, but after a while the light faded and it became difficult to see into the trees.

"Can't see nothin'," Robert whispered.

"Well, they ain't no better off," Henry whispered back.

"No they ain't," Joseph agreed. "You get them ears of yours working, Henry. I wanna know if a fly farts out there."

Henry nodded, a smile on his face.

The line settled into a silent watch as night swallowed the forest.

Several hours passed, and the darkness under the trees was complete. Joseph tried several times to check the watch, but he couldn't see the numbers clear enough to tell what time it was. He sighed and tried to think of something. He didn't want to light any torches and give the enemy something to shoot at. An idea popped into his head, and he reached into his pouch and pulled out a cartridge, then cleared an area on the ground as best he could.

"Whatcha doing?" Robert asked in a whisper.

"I need to see what time it is," Joseph whispered back. "I want you to hold this near the ground." He handed Robert the watch. Joseph tore open the cartridge and carefully poured the gunpowder on the ground. He took out his piece of flint and bayonet. "Keep it steady," he hissed.

Joseph scraped the edge of his bayonet along the flint, and sparks flew off the stone. One spark hit the tiny pile of gunpowder, igniting it. There was a brief flash of light as the powder burned, and Joseph saw the face of the watch. It lasted only a brief second, but it was enough. "Half hour before midnight," he muttered.

Henry crawled over and tapped Joseph on the shoulder. "I'm hearing some rustlin' in the bushes maybe fifty feet in."

Joseph peered over the berm. He held his breath and waited.

Finally, he heard a twig snap. He ducked back down.

"How can we shoot if we can't see 'em Joseph?" Robert asked.

Joseph thought about the watch. He groped for his pack and rummaged around. He pulled out one of his socks and laid it on his lap. "Give me some of your cartridges and tell the others to give some up too."

Robert and Henry handed over some of their ammo and went to get more. Soon Joseph had more than enough to work with. He began tearing open the paper sleeves and pouring the powder into his sock. "I need the boot strings from one of the dead soldiers." He continued to pour powder and the odd mini ball into his sock. Someone handed him a boot string and he laid it on the ground. Joseph carefully poured more powder onto the string and rubbed the powder into the lace with his fingers.

"Whatcha makin'?" Henry asked.

"Light," Joseph answered. "Tell the men to get ready to fire." Joseph tied the string around the neck of his sock, making sure one end was inside and the other end hung loose on the outside. He placed the sock on the ground and grabbed his flint and bayonet. He paused before striking the stone. "Everyone ready?"

There were several whispered yeses.

Joseph took a deep breath and slid the steel edge of the bayonet along the stone. Sparks flew away from the stone and lit the powder on the string. Joseph dropped the flint and bayonet, grabbed the sock, and threw it with all his might into the darkness. Then he grabbed his rifle and pulled the hammer to full cock.

There was a pause, and then the powder in the sock ignited. A huge flash splashed light against the faces of the Confederate soldiers trying to sneak up to the line.

"Fire!" Joseph yelled.

Everyone around him fired their weapons; soon the entire line was firing. The Rebels caught in the light fell under the hail of bullets. The Union soldiers firing into the dark were rewarded with screams of pain as some of their bullets found a mark.

Joseph could hear the retreating soldiers crashing into trees and through the underbrush. The sounds grew faint, and soon they were left in silence again. "I reckon we won't be seeing them until tomorrow." He sat down heavily on the ground. "Have the second watch stay ready. The first watch can sleep if they have a mind. Pass it on."

Joseph sat for a bit, then pushed himself to his knees and leaned against the top of the berm. He rested his rifle along the top and closed his eyes, trusting his ears in the darkness to warn him of any approach.

He stayed that way through the night.

13

FRIDAY, MAY 6, 1864

SECOND DAY OF BATTLE OF WILDERNESS

Robert "Joseph? You want some coffee"

Joseph blinked his eyes and yawned. He had remained at the wall the entire night, and his back and legs were burning from kneeling in the same position for so long. He turned and saw Robert crouching with the pot held out. Little curls of steam wafted from the pot, and Joseph caught the strong aroma of coffee.

Joseph "That smells good," he said, reaching into his pack for his tin cup. He held it out and Robert filled it. "Everyone doin' okay?" Joseph stretched his legs out as much as he could in the narrow ditch and sighed.

Robert "Tired, is all," Robert answered. "I don't think anyone got much sleep."

"I hear ya," Joseph said before taking a couple of deep swallows of his coffee.

The lieutenant moved along the ditch, making small talk with the men and patting them on the back with encouraging words. He stopped and sat down when he reached Joseph. "That was quite the night."

"Yes, sir." Joseph reached into his coat and retrieved the watch, handing it back to the lieutenant. "Robert, get the lieutenant a cup."

Robert hurried off and returned with a cup of coffee for the lieutenant.

"Thank you."

"Any word from headquarters?" Joseph asked.

"A runner came in this morning. The Rebels are massing more men at the clearing. Looks like they'll try another charge soon."

"I'll let the men know."

The lieutenant took a sip of coffee and grimaced.

"Sorry about the coffee," Joseph said.

"No, it's fine enough. It's hot. Gets the blood warmed up." He gave Joseph a hard look. "We need to hold this line."

"We'll do our best."

"Good." The lieutenant handed the cup back to Robert and headed back down the line.

"Dump the coffee and pick up your rifle."

Robert smiled. "I could serve Johnny Reb some of my coffee. They'd surrender right quick." He poured the pot out over the edge of the berm and went back to grab his rifle.

Joseph scanned the trees and underbrush. The silence had deepened, and the hairs on the back of his neck stood up. "Get ready, men! Fix bayonets!"

Suddenly, the woods were filled again with rebel yells as a wall of gray uniforms pushed out from the trees. Joseph could clearly see their numbers had increased.

"Fire!"

The wall fell, but a second wall rolled over the dead and dying alike and continued forward. Joseph moved back, and the second line aimed their rifles.

"Fire!"

Again, the wall collapsed and again it was replaced. The Confederates gained ground with each advance. Joseph finished reloading and moved to the berm.

"Fire at your convenience!" He took aim and fired; moved back and reloaded; moved to the front and fired.

The Confederates were taking heavy casualties and their advance slowed, but here and there along the line, small pockets of Rebels managed to reach the earthworks.

Joseph could hear men yelling and the clanking of bayonet against bayonet as hand-to-hand fighting erupted at points along the Union position. He moved along the line and helped push the enemy back from the trench.

The fighting was heavy, and several times it looked to Joseph as if the line would break, but each time the men held and managed to push the Confederates back. They eventually tired and, depleted of men, they turned and ran back into the trees.

Joseph leaned against the berm, his breath coming in heaves. Henry approached, and Joseph saw that he was limping. The right leg of his trousers was torn and stained bloody.

Henry

"It's just a scratch," Henry said, waving any questions away. "We almost lost it that time."

Joseph wiped sweat from his forehead. "You'll get no

argument from me." He pointed behind Henry. "How many?"

"We lost almost half," Henry answered. "Six dead, ten wounded. Of those, four won't make it to the end of the day."

Joseph grimaced. The losses were heavier than he had hoped, but still less than he had feared. "Make sure any man that can still hold his rifle is reloaded and at the line."

"And the others?"

"They'll have to stay where they are. We can't spare the men right now to move 'em."

Henry spat over the short wall. "Glad *you* got the stripes." He turned and headed back down the trench.

The rest of the morning, the two forces traded sporadic fire, but no charge came. The sun moved past noon, and suddenly the forest was filled with the familiar yelling.

"Here they come!" Joseph hollered. "Fire!"

Several Confederate soldiers fell, but not enough to stop the wave of men from plowing through the trees. Joseph saw the entire right flank of the line collapse. He reloaded and realized that the enemy was only fifty feet away. "Robert! Henry, Jerome! Move!"

Joseph turned and ran through the bush behind the trench. He was joined by the others. He could hear the Rebels yelling as they overtook the berm.

Joseph turned to see Henry lagging behind, the wound in his leg binding the muscle. He ran back with Jerome, and the two held him up as they continued on. They had traveled several yards when the front of Henry's chest exploded as a mini ball entered his back and sped out his front.

Henry fell to the ground, dead. Joseph stopped to pick him up, but Jerome grabbed the collar of his coat and yanked him away.

Jerom "He's dead!" Jerome yelled.

They caught up with Robert and stumbled into a small clearing. They paused to catch their breath, but the sound of men crashing through the underbrush reached them.

Joseph dropped to one knee and pointed his rifle at the trees. "Jerome, you and Robert scout ahead a bit. Find someplace we can hide."

Robert and Jerome nodded and moved at a crouch into the trees ahead.

Almost immediately, Joseph heard the sound of gunshots and Robert came running back. "They shot Jerome," he half sobbed.

The noise was now all around them.

Robert "Joseph?"

Robert Joseph looked at Robert, his young face stretched and pale. "It ain't that I'm afraid of dying," Robert said. "I just don't want to die today." He cocked his rifle and held it ready. "Tell me what to do, Joseph. I'll do it."

The sound of the approaching men closed in on them. Joseph looked at his friend's face and smiled. He lowered his rifle to the ground and motioned for Robert to do the same. He raised his hands as Confederate soldiers burst into the clearing.

Josep "We live."

SATURDAY, MAY 7, 1864

THE JOURNEY SOUTH

Joseph sat with his back to the wall of the railcar, his knees drawn up close to give room to the other prisoners around him. He flared his nostrils at the stench that clung to everything. It wasn't just the smell of unwashed bodies and uniforms that made his stomach clench. He was used to that. It was the stench of festering wounds coming from some of the prisoners, along with the piles of vomit that covered almost the entire floor of the car.

He turned his head and managed to get a bit of fresh air coming in from the cracks in the wooden planks that made up the walls. The same cracks allowed a bit of light to filter in and illuminate the interior enough to make out the faces around him. Luckily, most of the other prisoners were asleep from exhaustion and illness.

He put a hand into his jacket and felt the diary still concealed there. When he and Robert had surrendered, the soldiers had taken their rifles and ammo pouches, but after giving their haversacks a quick going through, they concerned themselves more with the food rations than with searching their uniforms.

The soldiers marched them east and south until they reached the Orange Turnpike. They had set up an area for the prisoners, and soon Joseph and Robert were milling about with other Union soldiers. They spent the day there before being marched out to the rail lines, where they were packed into the cattle cars.

Joseph looked around the car and found another sergeant close by. The man looked to be far older than he, but Joseph realized that looks were deceiving. War seemed to age men, and everyone in the car was covered in the dirt and soot of battle.

"Hoover of the 121st New York," he said, holding out his hand.

"Johnson, 118th Pennsylvania," the man said, shaking Joseph's hand. "I guess it's over for us."

"Yeah, I reckon so. Any idea where they'll be takin' us?"

"I'm guessing Andersonville." The sergeant saw one of his own and gave a wave. "We got word that they was building a new prison there."

"New doesn't sound bad," Joseph said.

Johnson barked a laugh. "You're young. You might survive the prison camp. But if I was you, I'd pray for early parole."

"What makes you say that?"

"This is my second time being captured." The sergeant began coughing violently. He spat on the floor of the car, and Joseph saw that it was black. "From eatin' too much gunpowder, I reckon," the sergeant said, noticing Joseph's gaze.

"When were you captured?" Joseph asked.

"Last year, at the Jones Crossroads. Spent the better part of six months at Salisbury." The sergeant started coughing again. He finally stopped and spat up another black glob.

"How did you get back? Escape?"

"Got traded for a captain," Johnson answered. "I got lung fever whilst in the prison camp, and they had pity on me, I guess. Probably figured I'd not live long 'nough to get back into the war." He barked another laugh that led to more coughing.

"Maybe they'll trade you again," Joseph said encouragingly.

Johnson shook his head. "Those six months nearly put me in the grave. I ain't foolin' myself. I don't expect to last out the month at Andersonville."

Joseph didn't know what to say.

Johnson pulled his knees up. "I don't mean to be rude, but I think I'll try and get some sleep."

"Of course," Joseph said. He turned his head away and looked at Robert, asleep on his right. Joseph made a silent promise to make sure that he and Robert survived the prison camps long enough to be paroled or traded.

He glanced around the car and saw that most were either asleep or keeping to their own. Joseph reached into his coat and pulled out his diary and pencil. He laid the book against his knees to hide it from anyone that might look and began writing. He kept an eye for anyone taking an interest and managed to get a couple of lines down before closing the book and hiding it back inside his coat.

He turned his attention back to the crack in the boards and tried to watch the land pass by. He couldn't help but feel anxious as each passing second brought him farther and farther south into enemy territory.

Robert "You awake, Joseph?"

Joseph swung his head around and saw that Robert had woken. "Yeah."

Robert rubbed his eyes and tried to stretch his legs without hitting bodies. "Where are we?" He yawned.

Joseph shook his head. "South is 'bout all I can figure. And heading deeper into it <u>fast</u>."

Robert "What do you think it will be like?" Robert asked.

Joseph glanced over at Johnson. The older sergeant had passed out, his head swaying back and forth with the motion of the car. Joseph saw black drool at the corner of the man's mouth and thought about what they had talked about. "I expect it shouldn't be any worse than our own camp," he lied.

Robert "Maybe better," Robert said. "We won't have to drill."

Joseph smiled. "I reckon not."

Robert "When do you think they'll feed us?"

"Most likely, they won't be handin' out rations until tomorrow. Best try to sleep so you won't be worryin' about it."

Robert "Wonder what they call 'rations' down here?"

Joseph "Can't be any worse than hardtack," Joseph answered.

Robert laughed. "Wouldn't it be somethin', Joseph, we travel to the Deep South and find out they got hardtack there?"

Joseph "Yeah. Somethin'."

Robert put his head down on his arms and let the rocking of the car lull him to sleep.

Joseph laid his head back and closed his eyes, but sleep would not come. He opened his eyes and turned his head. Johnson was staring at him.

"Why'd you lie to the kid?"

"How bad is it?" Joseph asked, ignoring the question.

"Bad," Johnson answered. "I ain't claimin' to know what Andersonville is like, but it can't be better." Johnson coughed again. "Like I said, you two are young and strong. You stand a chance, I reckon."

"You made it through once," Joseph said. "How?"

"Find others from your regiment. If there's none, find some from your state. Stick together. You won't starve as bad if you group together and share the garbage they give you to eat. It'll seem like you're starvin', and I guess you are. Just slower."

"Thank you," Joseph said.

"I saw you writin' in that little book of yours."

Joseph stiffened and put a hand to his coat. "What about it?"

"Paper," Johnson answered. "It's worth more'n you could think. You can trade some of it for food or corn mash from the guards, if that's your druther." Johnson laughed, resulting in more coughing. "I'd take the mash if I was you. Keep you numb."

"It's my diary," Joseph whispered. "I need to keep it."

Johnson shrugged. "Suit yerself. Best keep it safe, then. There are those that would kill you for it and not lose a wink of sleep."

"Thank you for the warning."

"Ain't no skin off my nose." Johnson turned his head to spit. "One thing you should get straight in yer head."

"What's that?"

"Men can change in prison. You might think 'cause you're on the same side that they'll all be friendly, but it ain't so."

Joseph looked at the men around him. "You're sayin' I can't trust anyone?"

Johns "No, I ain't sayin' that. But you need to listen to me. On the outside there was good soldiers and bad. I'm sure you know this."

Joseph nodded.

"Well, you pen thousands of soldiers together, good and bad, and then starve 'em, well, the bad get worse and some of the good get bad."

Joseph frowned. He hadn't thought about having to protect Robert and himself from both the guards and soldiers from his own side. "You're not leavin' me with a lot of hope."

Johnson shrugged again. "It's best you know the worst. You go in all wide-eyed and innocent, you won't last out the week." He pointed at the sleeping Robert. "Especially him. They'll chew him up and bury his bones faster than you can say 'as you please.'"

Joseph "Why are you telling me this?" Joseph asked.

Johns "You seem decent enough," Johnson answered. "My first time in I got the same speech I'm givin' you. It kept me alive. I'm doin' the Christian thing and passin' it on."

Joseph "My thanks," said Joseph. "I can't say you've made me feel better 'bout where we're going, but I can see you mean well enough."

Johns "Just remember what I told you." Johnson started coughing again. It went on for some time before it finally subsided enough for the man to talk. "You got family?"

Joseph "Yes," Joseph answered.

Johnso "I got an older brother. He's married with kids."

Joseph "That's nice."

Johnso "I ain't tellin' you this for the sake of conversation," Johnson wheezed. "We're headin' to the same place, but I know I ain't makin' it out. If you make it back, I want you to send word to him. His name is Daryl Johnson. He has a farm just south of

Hagerstown."

Joseph "I'll remember," Joseph assured the man. "Maybe you'll make it back yourself."

Johnson laughed and hacked some more. "Maybe."

They both stopped talking, and the car was filled with the clacking of the train wheels.

Johns "No matter how I go," Johnson said quietly, "you'll tell him I died well. If I'm lying in my own puke, wailing and sobbin' like a baby, you tell 'em I died like a man."

Joseph swallowed hard. "I will," he said. "I promise."

That seemed to satisfy the sergeant, and he lowered his head to his knees and fell back asleep.

They spent the next several days either sleeping and waking in the train car or lying on the ground outside, under guard. The train broke down on one occasion, and they were kept in the cars until another train was brought up the next day. The new engine was attached to the cars, and they continued south. Joseph made sure, anytime they were moved from the car, that he, Robert, and Sergeant Johnson stayed together.

It wasn't until their third day of captivity that rations were finally handed out. By that time everyone was starving. Johnson was too weak to stand in line for food, so Joseph made sure he got his share of the rations.

Robert "I swear, Joseph, I could eat squirrel raw I'm so hungry," Robert said around a mouthful of soft bread.

Joseph "You'd have to fight me for it." Joseph grinned. He stuffed more of the bread into his mouth. It wasn't much, but it felt good just to chew again, and the bread would at least muffle the sounds coming from his stomach. He tore off more bread and handed it to Johnson.

Johns "You know, you could just keep my share of the rations," Johnson said as he took small bites from the bread. "I reckon it's wasted on me." He coughed up more black.

Joseph "Whether you make it or not, well, that's in God's hands. You starving is in my hands, and I'll not sit here watching you get thinner than a rail spike."

"Suit yerself."

Johns A fight broke out in the far corner of the car. Two men began wrestling over the rations. It took several men to separate them, and by then the bread they had been fighting over had disappeared.

Johns "You'll see that happen more and more," Johnson said quietly. "Bread now, boots and blankets later. After a few months they'll be fighting 'cause there's nothing else to do."

Joseph "What about the guards?" Joseph asked. "Won't they stop the fighting?"

Johns "Some will. Others look at it different. If they get killed, less prisoners to guard. More rations for them."

Joseph stared at the corner where the two men sat nursing their wounds.

Johns "Remember what I said about that book of yours," Johnson said under his breath. "They will kill you for it."

Joseph "I'll remember." Joseph felt the outside of his coat.

The next day brought a new kind of misery for Joseph and the other prisoners.

Rain.

Joseph looked at the ceiling of the railcar, wondering why they'd even bothered to put a roof on. The wooden planks had warped and cracked over the years, and the water came pouring in almost unhindered. There wasn't a spot in the car that provided anything resembling dry, and soon everyone was soaked and shivering.

Joseph looked over at Johnson and saw that the sergeant had slumped down and his face was lying in water. He grabbed the man's coat and pulled him back to a sitting position and tried to wake him. He felt the man's face and realized he was burning with fever. "Robert! Give me your blanket."

Robert unrolled his blanket and handed it to Joseph.

"We need to try and keep the rain off him." Joseph stuffed one side of the blanket into a crack between two boards of the wall behind Johnson. He looked around for something to prop up the other side to form a loose tent over the sergeant's body.

One of the other men managed to tear up a section of floorboard and handed it down the line to Joseph.

Robert grabbed the piece of board and wedged it into another crack in the floor, allowing Joseph to stretch the blanket over Johnson's body. He unlaced one of his boots and used it to tie the blanket to the board Robert had wedged to the floor.

"Stuff the other edges into the floor if you can," Joseph told Robert. Between the two of them, they managed to keep most of the rain off the sergeant. The blanket soon became soaked, but the water drained down the sides to the floor.

Joseph sat cross-legged at the open end of the blanket and kept a watch on Johnson throughout the rest of the day.

"How's he doing?" Robert asked, moving to sit next to Joseph in the afternoon.

"Not so good." Joseph took off his kepi and ran his fingers through his wet hair. "He's burnin' with fever, and I don't know what to do."

Robert glanced into the tent and saw the man moaning

133

softly in his sleep. "Is he dying?" *Robert*

Joseph "I think so. I think he was dying before we got put on the train."

Robert sat there with his friend, not knowing what to do or say.

The afternoon darkened into evening, and finally the rain let up. Joseph wrinkled his nose at the stench that now filled the car. The rain did little to cleanse the area; instead it seemed to magnify the smell, making it thicker.

Robert "Try to get some sleep, Joseph." Robert put a hand on his friend's shoulder. "I'll keep watch."

Joseph nodded and moved to rest his back against the wall of the railcar. It took only a few seconds before he fell into a deep sleep.

Next session "Joseph? Joseph! Wake up."

Joseph opened his eyes and saw Robert hovering over him. He pushed himself to a sitting position and rubbed his eyes. *So* "How long have I been asleep?"

Rob "Hard to tell in this box," Robert said. "Few hours, I reckon." He handed Joseph a sandwich made from two thick slices of bread with strips of bacon piled in between. "They handed out rations a while ago. I managed to save you this."

Joseph took the sandwich and bit into it. The salty bacon made his mouth pucker, but it tasted good and he chewed slowly. "How's Johnson doing?"

"He stopped moaning and thrashing about, but his fever is still with him."

Joseph swallowed. "I don't know if that's good or bad." He quickly ate the rest of the bread and bacon before moving to the open end of the tent. He peered inside and saw the Sergeant lying on his side. At first, Joseph couldn't tell if the man was breathing and for a brief second thought the worst, but then he saw Johnson's chest move in and out slightly. "He's still breathing."

They remained on the train for several more days, making stops along the line for fuel and rations. Joseph managed to get food into Johnson each time he woke, and after a week the sergeant was able to sit up and eat on his own.

They had left the train and were staying at an old prison while they waited for another train to take them the rest of the way to Andersonville. Joseph had found an empty cell and had some of the men carry the sergeant inside. A Confederate doctor had visited the prison and looked at Johnson for a minute.

"What can you do for him?" Joseph asked after they had left the cell.

"Nothing to be done, son," the doctor said. "The fever's abated for now, but it's deep in his lungs. My advice is to make him as comfortable as possible, considering your situation, and pray."

"These Southern sawbones ain't worth much, are they?" Robert said after the man had left.

"I reckon he's got other concerns," Joseph sighed. He looked back at the cell door. "We'll do as he says. Maybe, good Lord willin', he'll get better."

"His breathin' ain't right, Joseph," Robert said. "If you listen close, it sounds almost like he's full of water."

Joseph changed the subject. "Are they passing out rations?"

"I'll go check." Robert trotted off, leaving Joseph on his own.

Joseph looked around and saw that a lot of the men were looking at him. He felt suddenly exposed for some reason and headed back into the cell.

"How you feelin'?" Joseph asked. He sat next to Johnson and put his hand on the man's forehead. "Your fever's down."

Johnson's chest heaved, and a terrible, rattling cough shook his whole body. He leaned over on his side and spat up more black onto the floor.

Joseph waited until the coughing subsided. "How you feelin'?" he asked again.

"I feel as if the entire Northern army marched over me." Johnson said. His voice was weak and his breathing rattled in his chest. "Where are we?"

"An old prison." Joseph brought his canteen over and let Johnson drink his fill. "How far from Andersonville, I can't say."

"Don't be in a rush to get there, Hoover."

Joseph laughed. "I reckon my days of rushin' around are over. Leastways for now." He sat back and rested against the wall of the small cell.

"Reach down into my right boot," Johnson said.

Joseph did as he was told and pulled out a folding knife.

"Take it. It'll come in handy where you're goin."

"You sure?"

Johnson waved the question away.

Joseph stashed the knife in his haversack. "Thank you," he said.

Robert returned with his haversack full. "I was able to talk the guards into giving me a bit more. Told 'em I was bringin' rations back for a couple of sick soldiers."

"What did they give you?" Joseph shifted his legs to a kneeling position.

"We have cornbread, bacon, and"—he held up a lidded tin— "bean soup." He handed the tin to Joseph. "It's still warm."

Joseph held the tin up to Johnson's face. "Can you eat a little?"

The sergeant nodded and took a few small gulps of the soup, then laid his head back. "Not bad for Southern fare." He shook his head when Joseph held the tin up again. Johnson closed his eyes.

Joseph and Robert divided the rest of the food, Joseph making sure that some was set aside for Johnson should he want more later. They ate in silence. Joseph drank some of the bean soup and handed the tin over to Robert. "It's not bad," he said.

"We should do all right if they keep feeding us this," Robert said after taking a long pull at the soup. He wiped what dripped down on his chin with the sleeve of his coat.

Joseph glanced at the sergeant and remembered what he had been told. "Keep some of the bacon. I think we should try to put a bit aside every time they feed us."

Robert nodded and tucked a sliver of bacon in his clothing. Then they unrolled their blankets and spread them out on the floor of the cell.

"The guards said we'll be here at least one more day." Robert put his hands behind his head and stared up at the ceiling.

Joseph glanced over at the sergeant. "Good," he said. "He could use another day out of that coffin of a railcar." He closed his eyes. "We all could."

Joseph was jarred awake by the sergeant's screams. He rolled off his blanket and tried to grab Johnson's flailing arms. Robert moved to the sergeant's head and steadied it. "He's burnin' up again, Joseph."

"Johnson!" Joseph tried to rouse the man, but he was lost in the fever, and the best they could do was hold him down until his body lost its strength and finally lay still.

"Is he dead?" Robert asked.

Joseph knelt close and put his ear next to Johnson's mouth and nose. "No, he's still breathin', but just."

"What do we do?"

"I don't know, Robert. Reckon we wait it out."

They sat up the rest of the night. The sergeant moaned softly from time to time but lay still until morning. In the light they could see that the skin of his face had paled to a sickly hue except for around his eyes. His breath came in ragged gasps that would stop for several heartbeats before starting again. Several times Joseph thought he had taken his last, only to see his chest rise again. Robert left at first light to wander around the prison and talk to some of the other prisoners.

Joseph sat throughout the morning and watched the man's chest rise and fall, stop, and then rise and fall again. By early afternoon Johnson's chest stopped rising and falling for good. It took several minutes for Joseph to realize that he had finally taken his last breath.

Joseph closed the man's eyes and folded his hands over his chest. He laid his own hand on Johnson's and bowed his head.

Robert returned an hour later with more rations. He entered the cell and saw Johnson's body prepared as if in a coffin. He sat down heavily on the floor. "He's gone," he said quietly.

Joseph nodded.

"I don't know how to say this without it sounding cruel, but I'm glad."

"I understand what you mean," Joseph said. "He was sufferin' something fierce. He's found his peace."

There was a commotion outside the cell, and he heard raised voices.

"What's going on?" Joseph asked.

"We're being moved back to the train."

Joseph sighed. "Find a guard and let him know what's happened."

When Robert left the cell, Joseph gathered up what belongings the sergeant had and put them in his own haversack before the soldiers could get them. He knew they would keep whatever they found.

Joseph was standing outside the cell by the time Robert returned. He was followed by a couple of Confederate soldiers who pushed their way past once they reached the cell. "What'd he die of?" one of them asked.

"Fever," Joseph answered.

"Best get to the train."

Joseph nodded. He grabbed Robert and pulled him away from the cell when he saw what the soldiers were doing.

"Joseph! They's stealin' his boots!"

"Keep still!" Joseph hissed under his breath. "Make a fuss and they'll be stealin' ours." He dragged Robert along as they headed for the main doors of the building.

"It ain't right, Joseph."

"No, it ain't, but are you gonna tell 'em that? They'll gut you with their bayonets and say you was tryin' to escape." Joseph turned and looked him in the eye. "Listen to me. We're prisoners now. The place we're goin', we're gonna see a lot more, worse than this." He grabbed Robert's shoulders. "We keep our heads down from now on. We don't see anything; you understand?"

"But, Joseph—"

"No buts allowed. We keep our mouths shut. You understand?" Joseph gave Robert a quick shake. "Say you understand, Robert."

Robert lowered his head. "I don't rightly understand, Joseph, but I'll do as you say."

"Then let's get on the train." Joseph gently pushed Robert toward the lineup of Union prisoners waiting to climb into the railcars.

Joseph took one last look at the prison and saluted the sergeant.

15

TUESDAY, MAY 24, 1864

ANDERSONVILLE, GEORGIA, CAMP SUMTER

The train's brakes locked and the railcar was filled with the squealing of metal on metal as it shuddered and rocked violently back and forth. Joseph was tossed awake as he crashed into Robert's side and they both toppled over. Joseph pushed himself off Robert and sat there wondering what had happened.

Robert managed to get to his feet and stuck his face against a crack in the boards. "I think we're here, Joseph."

"Why do you say that?" Joseph rubbed his eyes before putting a hand to his coat, feeling for his diary. It had become a habit whenever he woke to check and make sure no one had taken it.

Robert moved his face around the crack, trying to get a

better look. "There's an awful lot of Rebs standing at attention, and I think I see an officer sittin' astride a horse."

Joseph sighed. "Well, at least we get out of this coffin they got us jammed into." He groaned as he got his legs under his body and stood up, then stretched the kinks out of his back. He tapped Robert on the shoulder and took his turn at the crack. "I reckon you're right. I think that's a captain on the horse."

The door to the railcar swung open, and daylight flooded the car, causing everyone to squint against the brightness.

"Get out, Union trash!" one of the guards yelled.

"Lot of nerve callin' us trash," Robert grated under his breath.

"Leave it be," Joseph warned. He slowly climbed down from the train and moved when a guard pushed him from behind with his rifle. Robert joined him, and they waited while the car emptied. Joseph looked up and down the train and saw hundreds of Union prisoners pouring out of the cars.

Joseph's eyes came to rest on the man on the horse. He looked to be in his thirties with black, short-cropped hair and beard.

The captain gave his horse a kick and moved past the guards. "I am Captain Henry Wirz. I am zee commandant of Andersonville Prison, known to you as Camp Sumter! Zose dat bear zee rank of sergeant vill get zee other prisoners to form ranks!"

The prisoners stood staring at the man.

The captain frowned and tugged at his beard. He nodded to a Confederate sergeant, who stepped forward and bellowed at the top of his lungs, "Those with the rank of sergeant will have the others form up in ranks."

Joseph turned and yelled at the soldiers near him. "Gentlemen! We are still soldiers! Form ranks! Let's show 'em what a Union soldier is!"

The men began moving around until they had more or less formed up into ranks resembling platoons. Joseph walked around the men, gently pushing and positioning them until he was satisfied, then returned to the front and stood at attention.

It took some time, but the several hundred prisoners finally resembled somewhat of an ordered group.

"Vell done!" said the captain. "You vill now march to your new home!"

Robert leaned forward and whispered to Joseph. "What part of the South is *he* from?"

"He's German," one of the guards who heard whispered back.

"Oh."

"Forward, march!" Joseph called out. He stepped out and heard the footsteps of the men following behind. Realizing that a lot of the men had not had much to eat the last few weeks, and some were still suffering from illness or wounds they had received from their last battle, he slowed his pace. He still felt pride that the men were marching at all, and he raised his chin as he passed by the captain.

They marched for a mile before rounding a corner and coming face-to-face with the first set of prison gates. Joseph led his group over a short bridge and through the gates. As they passed through, another set of gates opened, and he could see row upon row of tents in a huge field. It wasn't the sight that took his breath away. He had lived in a sea of tents for over two years. It was the stench that hit him like a punch. Even living in the confined space of the railcar for weeks did little to prepare him for the months of unwashed bodies and the waste that resulted from men living in tight quarters.

He had to clench his stomach to keep from vomiting.

Others were not so lucky, and dozens of men began throwing up as they passed through the inner gate.

Robert was one of the unlucky ones. "Ugh, Joseph!" he croaked. "What is that smell?"

Joseph looked around, and what he <u>couldn't</u> see outside the gates, he <u>saw</u> once he had entered the compound. The rows of tents sat in a combination of mud and human waste. "<u>Everything</u>," he answered. "It's the <u>smell</u> of <u>everything</u>."

They continued marching until the last man had crossed through. The guards shut the gates, and one of the Confederate sergeants addressed the prisoners.

(M) Reb Sarge "You will now line up in twos in front of that building over yonder." He pointed to a squat, whitewashed building in the north corner of the compound. "There you will be given a tent to share with a comrade of your choosing. If you do not have your tins and spoons on your person, you will be assigned one of each to share. The same goes for blankets. Rations will be portioned out in front of this same building each morning for two hours. Should you be late, then you shall go hungry. Do <u>not</u> be late." The sergeant took a couple of steps to stand near a single rail fence that stood waist high and ran completely around the inner perimeter of the compound. It created a space of twenty or so feet between it and the main wall of the prison.

The Sergeant patted the rail.

Reb Sarge "This is the deadline. Anyone attempting to cross this line will be shot by a marksman situated in one of these towers." The sergeant pointed at several towers around the high wall. "Should you even reach across the deadline, it will be considered an attempt to escape, and you will be shot." He left the rail and stood before the men again. "We will tolerate no riotous behavior or acts of rebellion. Both may be punished by being shot."

The sergeant paused to let the information sink in to the new prisoners. "You may now proceed to the building I have just acquainted you with." He stepped aside and motioned for the men to proceed.

Joseph pulled Robert along, and he managed to get to the head of the line. He stood with Robert as a couple of soldiers began placing items on an old wooden table. One of the soldiers motioned for them to approach.

"One tent with poles and rope," he sounded off.

Joseph grabbed the tent and tucked it under his arm.

"Do you have your tins and spoons?"

Both Joseph and Robert nodded.

"Blankets?" The soldier looked up and saw that both men had bedrolls strapped to their backs. "You'll want to guard those with your lives," he said, smirking. "Move along."

"What about rations?" Robert asked.

"If you missed this morning's distribution, then you shall have to wait until tomorrow morning."

"But we—"

Robert never got to finish. Joseph had seen the soldiers' glare and grabbed Robert by the collar, dragging him away.

"Are you trying to get a whuppin'?"

Robert pulled his coat out of Joseph's grasp. "It was worth a try."

"No, it wasn't," Joseph warned. "And we still have rations that we kept from before." Joseph began walking around the edge of the tents.

"What are we looking for?"

"Friends," Joseph answered. "We are going to need friends

to survive in here." He spotted a tight group of tents set apart from the others. There was a sign nailed to a piece of board that had a list of the regiments from Pennsylvania written on it.

Joseph led Robert on until he came to a similar group of tents that had been set on a patch of ground slightly higher than the rest of the field. Joseph read the sign aloud. "Twenty-fourth New York, Thirty-first New York, Seventy-second New York, and 122nd New York." Joseph stopped and smiled at Robert. "Friends," he said.

Joseph led the way to the tents and stopped in front of a group of eight men. Their uniforms for the most part seemed in decent condition. Only one of the men had sergeant's stripes. Joseph singled him out and stuck out his hand. "Sergeant Joseph Hoover, 121st New York Volunteers, C Company."

The man stared at Joseph without making a move to take his hand. Joseph remained standing with his hand out, his eyes never leaving the other's gaze. Finally, the man stepped forward and took the hand.

"Edward Breeze, 122nd, D Company."

"Pleased to meet you," Joseph said. "This is Private Robert Spencer, also of C Company. We were captured at the Wilderness almost a month ago."

Breeze nodded. "I'd expect you want to join our group."

Joseph smiled. "A fellow sergeant I met on the way here gave me some good advice. He'd been a prisoner before but got traded."

"He here now?" Breeze asked.

The smile melted from Joseph's face. "He died 'bout a week ago on the way here. Fever took him."

Breeze grunted. "Fever takes a lot of 'em. Here more than

any place else, as you'll soon find." He motioned with his hand to the men standing behind him. "Everyone here brings something to the fire." Breeze fell silent and waited.

"I can read and write," Joseph said.

Breeze shrugged his shoulders. "Me and three others here can read and write. Who do you think made the sign?"

Joseph hesitated. He looked inside his haversack and found Johnson's things he had taken from the cell. He hadn't bothered to look through them until now. He found a deck of worn cards tied with a length of twine and the knife Johnson had given him. "I have this," he said holding out the folding knife.

There were low murmurs of approval from the men.

"We can always use another knife," Breeze said. "Anything else?"

Joseph pulled out the pack of cards, thinking they wouldn't be much good. "This," he said, tossing the cards to Breeze.

The men moved forward and crowded around the Sergeant. "Now, that's somethin', ain't it Sarge? We haven't had a set of cards since we got robbed," one of the younger men said excitedly.

Breeze held the deck up to Joseph. "You willin' to share?"

"Keep 'em."

Breeze looked genuinely surprised. He handed the cards to one of the men. "Okay. Welcome to New York." He looked at Robert. "What about you?"

Robert tilted his head at Joseph. "I'm with him."

Breeze barked a laugh. "All right." He pointed behind him. "Find a spot to pitch your tent. When you're done, we'll have a talk."

Joseph and Robert made their way between the men,

nodding and shaking their hands. They found a spot and set up their tent, tossing their bedrolls inside.

They found Breeze and the others sitting around a fire, a rather large cast iron pot hovering over the flames. One of the men, the young one who got excited over the cards, was putting bits of meat into the pot. It took Joseph a second to remember the man's name. "Looks good, Tim," he said. The younger man smiled.

Breeze motioned for the others to make room, and Joseph and Robert sat down on the ground.

Breeze "You missed rations this morning, but we got enough for tonight."

Robert smiled and began pulling out sections of cornbread and thin slabs of salted pork.

Breeze "Looks like you do have something to bring to the fire," Breeze said.

Robert got up and stood over the pot. He reached into his haversack and started scooping out handfuls of rice. "It'll thicken the stew." He handed Tim the bacon and sat back down.

Joseph "They fed us pretty good on the train." Joseph picked up the cornbread and broke off a small piece and handed the rest to Breeze.

Breeze took a piece and handed it off. "Well, looks like we done broke bread together."

Joseph "Reckon so."

Breeze cleared his throat. "We got simple rules here," he announced. "We don't steal from one another, and we share our rations. Everything we get goes into the pot."

Joseph "Sounds fair," Joseph said.

Breeze "I'd prefer it that you don't go stealin' from any of the other soldiers. It's tempting, but it brings unwanted attention to us, and the punishment for getting caught by the Rebs is pretty harsh. Worse if you get caught by our own."

"Sounds smart." Joseph chewed on his piece of cornbread.

"We don't leave less than three of us guarding the tents during the day," Breeze said. "It would be good if you could leave your knife with anyone standin' guard."

"I can do that," Joseph agreed. "Does that happen often?"

"It's happened twice to us. We managed to fight them the second time, but the first time they managed to get some clothes and our deck of cards." Breeze pointed at Tim. "Tim got his nose broke trying to protect 'em."

Tim smiled and Joseph saw the crooked angle of his nose.

"They're called Raiders, and every camp has 'em. You'll see 'em soon enough." Breeze finished his cornbread and burped. "How's the stew comin'?"

"Be ready soon, Sarge." Tim bent over the pot and stirred the contents. "The rice ain't quite done."

Breeze grunted and addressed Joseph again. "Don't ever drink from the stream runnin' through the camp. Unless you wanna die of the fever. We got a deal going with some of the younger guards. They bring us fresh water from their own well, and we share some of our rations with 'em."

"Don't they get fed by their own?" Joseph asked, somewhat surprised.

"Take a good look at 'em," Breeze said. "They're either too old to fight or too young; they get the same rations we do."

Joseph took a long look at some of the guards nearby. One of the guards was barefoot, and they all had that hollow stare. He hadn't noticed it at first. "They're starvin'," he muttered.

Breeze "We leave enough in the bottom of the pot for two guards to eat. They leave us canteens of water."

Joseph "I can see what Johnson meant."

Breeze "Who's that?" Breeze asked.

Joseph "The sergeant I told you 'bout. The one that died of the fever. He told me to find friends once we got here. Safety in numbers."

Breeze "Huh. Smart man. Too bad he's dead. Could've used him."

Joseph "Yeah."

Tim "Food's ready," Tim called out.

Everyone took out their tins and handed them one by one to Tim, who filled them before handing them back. Joseph and Robert took out their spoons. Joseph put a hand on Robert's arm before he could get the first spoonful into his mouth.

Breeze "We say grace every night before we eat," Breeze said.

Joseph "Of course," Joseph said and bowed his head. Robert followed as the others bowed their heads and waited.

Breeze "Dear Lord," Breeze began, "we thank you for givin' us the strength to live another day in this place. Thank you for keepin' the fever from our tents and the Raiders off our backs. We thank you for our new companions and what they brought to this fire, and we thank you for the food. Amen."

A chorus of amens echoed.

Joseph spooned out some stew and shoved it into his mouth. He remembered what good food tasted like, and he knew that this food was far from what he got at home, but now, next to a fire and people he might be able to call friends, it was a feast fit for a king. He sighed as he swallowed.

Breeze "Hunger can make anything taste good," Breeze mumbled around a mouthful.

After eating, they sat around the fire, watching the rest of the camp. Union soldiers wandered past, some waving as they went, others lost in their own thoughts.

Tim pulled the deck of cards out and waved them at Breeze. "You any good at cards?" Breeze asked.

Joseph shook his head. "I'm not a gamblin' man."

Breeze shrugged. "It's not really gamblin' if you got no money. We play with pebbles." Breeze gave Joseph a strange look. "By the by, you wouldn't have any money, would you?"

Joseph shook his head. "We got paid out before the Wilderness, but I send my money home." Joseph looked over at Robert. "You got any?"

Robert pulled out three greenback dollars. "I got these."

Breeze looked at them. "You can either hang on to them or hand them over to Tim. He's our quartermaster of sorts. More of a scrounger, but he manages to get us stuff from the guards or from a group of prisoners that served under Sherman. They seem to get things inside the prison that no one else can, but you have to go to their tents. They're called 'stores.'"

"I'd rather deal with the guards," Tim chimed in. "Those tents attract the worst. 'Specially the gamblin' tents."

Robert looked at the bills in his hand and then handed them over to Tim.

Tim smiled and put the greenbacks in his pocket. "We can get a few sweet potatoes from the guards with these."

"I didn't think the Confederates used greenbacks," Joseph said.

"They don't," Breeze answered. "And it's a hefty punishment for them to be found carryin' 'em, but they can still use them as trade with other units headin' to the front lines. Sometimes Union and Confederate soldiers meet in secret and do a fair bit of tradin.'"

Joseph "I heard about that," Joseph said. He looked at the sky. It had deepened to a dark blue, and a few stars began to appear. *Joseph* "It's gettin' late. I'm gonna turn in if that's okay."

Breeze "Suit yerself," Breeze said. "We do night watches here. Every man takes a two-hour watch, but we'll let you and young Robert here sleep the night through. You can start doing watches tomorrow night."

Joseph "'Preciate that." Joseph got to his feet and headed for his tent.

Robert entered the tent a short time later. "I bet I could sleep for a week."

Joseph "I reckon we both could." Joseph rolled onto his side so he was facing his friend. "I think if we watch our step and keep with these folks, we'll be okay."

Robert "I never would have thought the camps would be this bad, Joseph." Robert said. "The prisoners, it's like they don't care how they're livin'."

Joseph "They've lost hope." Joseph said. "I can see it in their eyes." Joseph glanced out the tent to the fire, where the others were playing at cards. "Most of 'em, anyway. Men like Breeze and a few others seem to have made the best of it. He's a smart man. We'll do well to keep his company."

Robert nodded. He closed his eyes and soon fell asleep. Joseph tossed and turned for a bit but finally let sleep come.

Joseph and Breeze walked around the camp, keeping close to the outside but not too close to the deadline. He and Robert had been at Camp Sumter for almost two weeks, and each morning Breeze had taken his walk and invited Joseph to go with him.

At first the stench was almost unbearable, but after a couple of days, Joseph's stomach settled down and he no longer felt like retching. The sight of the men living in such conditions still made him wince inside, but Breeze seemed to not see it anymore.

Joseph stopped once to see a man, naked as the day he was born, shuffling along. He was so thin that Joseph could see the outline of the bones in his legs and arms, and the skin was stretched over his ribs. He shook his head and looked away.

Breeze "You get used to that," Breeze said. "There are some that have been here since the beginning. At first they hoped for parole or trade, but when it didn't come, I reckon they just gave up."

Joseph "Can't something be done?"

Breeze shrugged and continued walking.

Joseph turned and caught up to the man. "What about the commandant? Surely he's not blind to this?"

Breeze "You saw the guards your first day," Breeze reminded. "I reckon the Union's got the South in a pinch. Food and other supplies are short down here." Breeze waved his arms around. "Won't be long before we're all walking around like that man. Naked and starving." He glanced over at Joseph. "I know what you're thinkin'. Why don't we help that man?"

Joseph "I was thinkin' that."

"We can barely keep ourselves fed and clothed. We start helping everyone we see, won't be long before we need help." Breeze sighed. "I thought as you did when I first came here. My father's a preacher back home. This would break his heart."

Joseph "Will you ever tell him about this?" Joseph asked.

Breeze shook his head. "How can I? How can I tell him that his son looked away? Would you?"

Joseph "I reckon not."

Breeze "There's only three ways out of here," Breeze said as he put a hand on Joseph's chest to stop him. He pointed ahead. "You're about to see one of them."

Joseph looked where Breeze had pointed. A man almost as thin as the one before stood staring at the rail. His uniform hung in rags and he was barefoot. "What's he doin'?" Joseph asked.

Brez "Making a choice, I reckon."

The man began walking slowly toward the deadline.

Jos "Shouldn't we try to stop him?" Joseph asked.

Brez "It's too late."

The man reached the rail and placed a hand on the wood. He raised his leg as if to climb over, and the crack from a rifle filled the air. The man collapsed into the mud, his eyes staring at the sky.

The camp around them had become quiet as everyone turned to look at the man. A few seconds later, the noise of people talking and going about their business returned as if nothing had happened.

Joseph stood still, his heart pounding in his chest.

Brez "Come on," Breeze said. "We'll miss our rations."

Joseph "Are they just going to leave him there?"

Brez "Every morning at first light, the guards bring in a wagon. Those that died the day before or didn't make it through the night are brought out to the wagon."

Jose "So he'll lie there till tomorrow."

Breeze "He'll lie there till the morrow," Breeze repeated.

Joseph followed Breeze as they walked past the body and headed back to their tents. As they neared, Joseph could see several men standing in front of their tents. Robert and Tim were standing as if blocking the others' way.

Breeze began walking faster.

Joseph "What's wrong?" Joseph asked, keeping up.

Breeze "Raiders," Breeze growled. "The one in front, he's the leader."

Joseph watched as the leader of the group stepped up to Robert and punched him in the stomach. Robert crumpled to the ground. Everything around Joseph seemed to fade away save for the man who had struck his friend. He started running and launched himself at the man as soon as he drew near. He hit the man hard, and they both tumbled to the ground. Joseph got on top of the man and began striking him in the face with every ounce of strength he could muster.

Joseph could feel hands grabbing at him from behind, but he ignored them and continued to pummel the Raider until his face was a bloody pulp. Then he turned around and attacked another man, hitting him on the side of his head. The man collapsed to the ground. The rest began backing away.

Joseph stood with his fists raised. He was breathing hard, but he hadn't been at the prison long, and he was still healthy and strong. The others were easily cowed by the sight of Joseph's anger, and the ferocity of his attack shook their confidence.

Joseph pointed at the two men on the ground. "Take your men with you!" he grated between clenched teeth. "Come back here and you'll get more of the same."

Joseph stood where he was, scowling at the men as they picked up their fallen leader and comrade, and dragged them away. Joseph turned and helped Robert to his feet.

Joseph "You okay?"

Robert coughed, and he still held his stomach, but he managed a nod.

Tim "Never seen nothing like that before," Tim said. "You, Sarge?"

(to Breeze)

Breeze shook his head. "I reckon they won't be back for a while."

Joseph "You think they'll try again?" Joseph asked.

Breeze "Maybe. Maybe they'll just wait it out until you're alone and get some back. Either way it's gonna be a few weeks before Tanner can open his eyes again."

Joseph looked around. "What did they want?"

Tim shrugged. "What they always want. They want what we got." Tim looked at Breeze. "We heard a shot earlier."

Breeze nodded. "Someone climbed the deadline." He looked around. "Where are the others?"

Tim "Gone to get rations," Tim answered.

Breeze "Best we get there ourselves."

Joseph "Shouldn't we leave someone to guard?" Joseph asked.

Breeze "No one misses rations. It's after, when the weaker ones get their food, that they start the thieving."

Joseph grabbed Robert's arm. "You okay to walk?"

Robert "Yeah," Robert answered. "I shoulda seen that comin'." He looked at Joseph's coat. "They tore your jacket."

Joseph craned his neck over his shoulder and saw the seam at the shoulder had let go. "I'll fix it later. Let's get our food."

Joseph sat next to the fire with his coat spread out over his knees. He reached into his haversack and pulled out a small leather pouch his mother had given him before he left. It held a couple of bone needles and one shiny steel one, along with some black thread. He picked out the steel needle and pulled the thread through the eye.

He held the two edges of the tear between the fingers of his left hand and began sewing the seam back together.

Breeze "Strangest sight I ever saw," Breeze said as he watched Joseph repair his coat.

Joseph "What's that?" Joseph asked, not taking his eye off the work he was doing.

Breeze "You," Breeze answered. "Fightin' mad one moment, sittin' there sewing the next. Like nothin' happened."

Joseph shrugged.

Breeze "How's the hand?"

Joseph stopped and looked at the back of his right hand. The knuckles were scabbed over, and his middle finger was a bit stiff. He flexed his hand a couple of times. "Seems well enough," he said, returning to his sewing.

Breeze "That ever happen before?"

Robert "At Crampton's Gap," Robert answered. He had been sitting quiet most of the day, nursing his ego. "That was the first time. Joseph up and ran ahead of the charge. Never seen nothin' like it. He jumps over the fence, and Rebs start dropping like autumn leaves." He dipped his tin cup into the pot and drew out some coffee. "Next time was at Fredericksburg. Our sergeant said it was battle fever."

Joseph "If you gentlemen are finished discussing me . . ." Joseph tied off the thread and bit the end. He held the coat up and admired his handiwork. "Good as it'll get, I reckon." Joseph slipped his coat on and moved his arm about.

Breeze "Best you not go anywhere on your own for the next little while," Breeze said.

Joseph "I'll tag along with you," Joseph said with a slight grin.

Several weeks went by, and the heat of July made the conditions at the prison unbearable. The sun baked the grounds like an oven, and the stench overwhelmed even the toughest of stomachs. The only respite the prisoners had was at night, when the temperature dropped enough to make moving around possible.

Joseph lay in his tent during the afternoons. The others contented themselves with cards, but no one moved around much. Even the simplest of exertions caused them to sweat, and the water the soldiers brought at night was not enough to keep them from becoming dehydrated.

There was a commotion in the camp one day, and Joseph emerged from his tent to see what was happening. The others had stopped playing at cards and were looking toward the building where they got their rations. Ropes were being thrown over one of the big branches of the tree that stood nearby.

"Looks like they're gettin' ready to hang someone," Tim said.

"From the number of ropes they're tossing up, it looks like they're plannin' on hanging more than one." Breeze looked over at Joseph. "Let's take a walk. The rest of you stay put. The Raiders would use this to do their mischief."

Joseph and Breeze headed toward the building but soon had to push and shove their way to get close enough to see what was happening.

"It's those Raiders," Joseph said. He had spotted the leader, his face still bearing the marks of Joseph's attack.

The entire event took little time. A Confederate sergeant read out the charges and waved his hand. More soldiers hauled on the ropes, and the men, their hands tied behind their backs, were lifted off the ground by their necks. The ropes were tied off and the men left to dangle, their legs kicking for what seemed an eternity.

Joseph saw the men's faces begin to swell, and he turned away.

Breeze "They got what was comin' to them," Breeze said.

Joseph "I know," Joseph answered. "Doesn't mean I have to enjoy it nor watch it." He headed back to the tents, with Breeze walking slowly behind.

When they returned to their camp, Breeze gave the news to the others.

Tim "Well, that's a relief, and no doubt about it," Tim said, grinning.

Breeze "Six men are dead," Breeze said bluntly. "Nothin' to grin at."

Joseph stood a bit away from the group and looked out over the sea of human misery, wondering how much more any of them could take before all hope was lost. He shook his head and returned to his tent.

The summer moved along at a snail's pace for Joseph and the others. The camp was receiving more and more prisoners every week, and by September the camp was crowded to the point of bursting. The Confederates had begun to reduce the rations as the demands for food grew.

Joseph and Robert stood in line with Breeze and the others, waiting for their turn to collect their rations. A sergeant emerged from the building and called their attention as he read from a piece of paper.

Reb Sarge "Due to the increased population of the facility, six hundred prisoners have been chosen to be moved to another prison, from which they will be paroled."

The sergeant had to stop as the whole line erupted in cheers. When the soldiers had calmed down, he continued.

"When you come up to draw your rations, your name will be checked against the lists. Should your name be on said lists, you will make preparations to leave in the morning." He dropped the paper and looked at the men. "That is all."

Robert "You think our names are on that list?" Robert asked, his voice cracking with excitement.

Joseph "I don't know, Robert. They're only taking six hundred, and there's thousands here. I reckon they'd be looking at those that have been here longest." He looked around at the men and the horrible condition they were in. "A lot of these poor souls won't last much longer."

Robert looked disappointed. "I hadn't thought of that."

Joseph clapped his friend on the shoulder. "We'll get out of here. Mayhap they will do another list soon. I don't reckon they could fit more men here without having trouble keeping 'em in."

The line moved forward as each man gave his name to the sergeant. A few let out a holler before leaving, but most walked away with the realization that they had to stay.

Once he reached the front of the line, he received his rations and gave his name. "Sergeant Joseph Hoover, 121st New York."

The sergeant seemed to take forever, and Joseph began to *Reb serg* think that he would leave when the sergeant read his name from the list. "Hoover, make yerself ready to leave in the morning."

Joseph stood looking at the sergeant, stunned.

Reb sarge "Problem, boy?" the sergeant asked. He waved Joseph away. "We got lots of men to go through, and I ain't got all day."

Robert pushed Joseph aside and gave the sergeant his name. "Private Robert Spencer, 121st New York." He held his breath as the Sergeant checked the papers.

Reb Snx "Looks like it's your lucky day, son. Prepare to move out tomorrow."

Robert let out a holler and headed over to stand next to Joseph. His face was split with a wide grin. "We're goin' home, Joseph."

Joseph nodded, but his attention was focused on Breeze. The Sergeant checked the list and then shook his head.

"Can you check again?" Breeze asked. "Sergeant Edward Breeze, 122nd New York?"

The sergeant gave the sheets a cursory look but shook his head again. "Move along," he said.

Breeze turned away and walked past Joseph and Robert without saying a word.

"Come on," Joseph said. He walked behind Breeze back to the tents.

The others returned, all with downcast faces.

"Ain't fair, Sarge," Tim complained. "It ain't fair at all. We've been here longer."

"Fair's got nothin' to do with it," Breeze said. He looked at Joseph and Robert. "Congratulations," he said and held out his hand.

"They'll be doing up more lists," he said, shaking Breeze's hand. "They got too many men here."

Breeze nodded. "We'll be on the next one."

Joseph went to his tent and grabbed his haversack and Robert's as well. He carried them back to the fire. "You can have my stuff. The knife and sewing kit."

Robert looked in his sack and frowned. "All I got in here is some coffee grounds and a bit of rice." He held out the sack to Tim. "You can have the sack though."

Tim took the haversack and sat down.

The rest of the day dragged by, and the men sat or milled about in silence.

The sun rose into the afternoon, and Breeze stood up and motioned for Joseph to follow. They walked around the camp, not talking for a long time. Finally Breeze broke the silence.

Breeze "I won't lie to you, Joseph. I wish it was me headin' home instead of you."

Joseph "I know it."

Breeze "But I won't wish any man to remain here when he's got the chance to get out."

They continued walking.

Breeze "Could I ask you to get word to my folks?"

Joseph "I'd be glad to," Joseph said.

Breeze "Good," Breeze said. "Good." He looked at the sun. "We should head back. We can have our last meal together."

Joseph and Robert stood near the gate with the other six hundred prisoners. Joseph could see Breeze and the others standing near the building, watching.

The gates opened and the guards began moving the prisoners through the gates and out onto the road. Joseph took one last look and waved his hand as he left Camp Sumter.

Robert "What's the first thing you'll be doin' when you get home?" Robert asked.

Joseph grinned at the thought. "Eat a week's worth of food in one sittin'."

Robert laughed. "Sounds good. I think I'll do the same." He rubbed his stomach. "So long as it's not salted pork."

They laughed as they marched.

Joseph saw the train sitting on the tracks and the boxcars lined up behind. There was a moment of panic at the thought of having to get packed into one, but he reminded himself that it would be the last time.

The guards halted the men in front of the open cars; then

the order to board was given. Some of the men were too weak to climb in, so prisoners who were strong enough helped lift them into the cars. Joseph and Robert stood on either side of one door and helped those who needed it. When everyone was loaded, they climbed in and stood looking out at the country-side. Given any other circumstances, they would have thought the sight beautiful.

"I can't say I'll miss it," Robert said. He turned and started looking for a place to sit down.

One of the guards grabbed the door to pull it closed.

"Do you know where we'll be paroled from?" Joseph asked.

The guard regarded Joseph with a strange look on his face.

"There ain't going to be parole," he said. "They only told you that so's there wouldn't be any trouble movin' you all out."

The color drained from Joseph's face.

"Joseph?"

Joseph turned and looked at Robert.

"We ain't gettin' paroled?"

"No," Joseph whispered as the guard closed the door, cutting off the daylight and plunging the car into darkness.

16

MONDAY, SEPTEMBER 12, 1864

TRAIN TO FLORENCE, SOUTH CAROLINA

Joseph sat looking at the lines of light coming in from the cracks in the far wall of the car. After the news from the guard, Joseph drew inward, ignoring Robert's questions and attempts to talk.

The whole car was subdued. Joseph could hear some of the men quietly weeping in their hands; others merely rolled over on their sides, as if they had given up all hope. Joseph took out his diary and unwrapped the oilcloth that had kept it protected and opened it to the last page he had written. He rummaged around the inside pocket of his coat until he found the pencil and sat there wondering what he should write.

Joseph licked the tip of the pencil and wrote down two simple lines about taking the train south. He left out what had happened. If something should happen to him and his diary found its way home, he didn't want his mother to read anything despairingly about his circumstances.

Joseph wrapped the diary up and placed it back into his coat pocket. He looked around the car and spotted a man watching him intently. The man looked away and Joseph's attention turned to Robert, nodding next to him. A pang of sympathy went out to his young friend. His day had started with such hope, and then to have that smashed left him lost and confused.

The sound of movement brought his attention back to the man who had been staring at him. The soldier had begun to make his way across the floor of the car. Joseph watched as the man took pains not to disturb the men who lay sleeping.

"Joseph?" Robert had opened his eyes and sat up but had not seen the man crawling along the floor toward them.

"Yes, Robert?" Joseph kept his eye on the approaching man.

"Do you think we'll ever see freedom again? The end of this war?"

"I don't know, Robert. I reckon so. It can't last forever."

Robert dropped his head in his hands. "We were supposed to be paroled. Not sent to another prison."

"That's the truth."

"I mean, this ain't no way to treat men. Keepin' us penned up like cattle and shippin' us around like we was animals." Robert raised his head and looked at Joseph. "This ain't the kind of war I signed up for."

"I don't think you ever really sign up for a certain kind of war. I didn't have any notions as to what kind of war it was. It just happens the way it happens." Joseph sat up straighter and gave Robert a nudge.

The man finally reached them. "Well, how does this do for so-called Southern hospitality?"

Joseph didn't answer. The man looked cocky to him, his kepi sitting on his head at an angle that looked like it would fall off.

Tom "I'll tell you what," the man continued. "I much prefer Virginia to this." He waved his hands around. "The whole damn lot of 'em down here can rot in hell for all I care." He smiled and gave Joseph's knee a light punch. "What say we get on out of here so we can show 'em where they can put it?"

Robert "Put what?" Robert asked, half smiling at the man.

Tom "Why, their 'hospitality,' of course. Quite the difference here, if you ask me."

Joseph "What hospitality are you talkin' of? We're prisoners, if that has slipped your mind."

The man smirked at Joseph. "My word. We have ourselves a perfesser here."

Joseph scowled at the man.

Tom "No offense intended," the man said quickly, holding up his hands. "Apologies. I was just tryin' to break the tension of the situation." He sat down. "Feels good to stretch the legs, though, so to speak. Don't it?"

Robert "At least we ain't in Andersonville anymore." Robert sat back. "It can't be worse where we're goin'."

Tom "Say, either of you boys got half a tent?"

Joseph "No," Joseph answered. "Wasn't expectin' to have use for it."

Tom "You?" the man asked Robert.

Robert "No."

"Well, then ain't you in luck, 'cause I just happen to have two halves, which make up a whole, if you know what I mean.

It's a bit ragged, mind you, but it'll do in a pinch."

Robert "You got a name?" Robert asked.

The man smiled like he had hooked a fish in some secret watering hole. "'Course I got a name. Don't we all? I know fer certain that's one of the requirements to muster in." He stuck out his hand. "Thomas J. Ryan, corporal with the Seventeenth Maine Volunteer Infantry." His smile seemed to get bigger. "Youse can call me Tom. And you, sirs?"

Robert took the hand. "Robert Spencer. Private with the 121st New Yorkers. This is Sergeant Joseph Hoover of the same regiment."

Tom held his hand out to Joseph and gave him a wink.

Joseph looked at the hand and at the man offering it. Given what had happened at the camp, he eyed the man with suspicion.

Tom kept his hand out, waiting patiently.

Joseph finally took the hand and gave it a brief shake.

Tom "I seen you a few times back at the camp," Tom said. "You and Robert here kept with the other New Yorkers."

Joseph "Yeah?"

"Just sayin' it was smart. I myself floated around a bit. Started out with the Pennsylvanians, then moved over with the boys from Michigan." Tom pointed at Joseph. "I even saw what you did to that Raider leader and his buddy." He tilted his head. "That was somethin' to see."

Joseph "You headed somewhere with this?" Joseph asked.

"Look, I'm the only one from my company that got captured during one particularly unpleasant meeting with the Rebs." He moved closer so he could lower his voice. "And on account of some unfortunate debts I honestly incurred, I didn't exactly leave Camp Sumter with a lot of friends."

Joseph   "So to speak," Joseph quipped sarcastically.

"Sounds strange, I know, given my friendly disposition, but I'd feel better if I could stick with someone I knew whilst we was stuck in the same situation."

Joseph   "So to speak." Joseph frowned.

Robert   "I suppose it'd be all right," Robert said. "What do you say, Joseph?"

Joseph looked at Robert like he'd lost his mind.

Robert   "Safety in numbers," Robert reminded his friend.

Joseph sighed. "I reckon so."

Tom clapped his hands together and rubbed them. "Good. That's settled, and my thanks, gents." Tom put his back to the end wall of the car and tilted his kepi over his eyes.

The next couple of days were a mix of long stretches of horrible heat during the day and bracing cold at night. Tom did his best to entertain Robert with tales of his antics during training and the time spent between battles. Even Joseph found himself smiling at some of the stories, and it was good to hear young Robert laugh. Joseph spent most of the time looking at the landscape passing by through the cracks in the boards. He saw acres and acres of white cotton fields that looked eerily like the fields in winter back home.

At one point the man sitting next to him slid over to come to rest against Joseph's shoulder. Joseph shook the man gently before realizing he had died in his sleep. Joseph pushed the man carefully away and laid him down on the floor of the railcar. The most he could do for the dead man was to compose his arms across his chest and close his eyes.

Nights gave Joseph little comfort in the way of sleep. He maintained his vigil at the crack and napped sporadically, always waking up a short time later to watch the shadows of trees and the odd building pass by. He could see some of the stars and once stared at the moon for hours before it finally moved to the other side of the train.

Tom "What do you see out there?" Tom asked one night.

Joseph turned away from the crack and saw Tom looking intently at him. Despite the darkness of the car, Tom's eyes almost glowed. Joseph returned to looking out the crack. "I see a world passing away without us. Everything we fought for, everything we sought to do for our country, passing away, and now we won't have much to do about any of it."

Tom "What did you do before the war?" Tom asked.

Joseph "I was a farmer."

Tom "You sound as if you don't consider yerself a farmer anymore," Tom said.

Joseph "I reckon I don't know what I am anymore. I know I'm not the same person that started out from his farm more'n two years ago." Joseph slumped against the wall, his mind focusing on memories of home. "I don't even know if I can go back when all this is over, or if I'll even live to see it. Hell, I don't even know what day it is."

Tom "Well, we ain't rottin' in that camp anymore, and that's gotta be invigorating."

Joseph "What does that have to do with anything?" Joseph asked, annoyed with the man's seemingly carefree attitude.

Tom "We're outside, moving, and moving means things are changing, and for me that means one more step closer to freedom."

Joseph grunted a short laugh and shook his head. "We're in a Confederate prison train heading deeper and deeper into enemy territory. Movin' from one prison to another. The only thing that could possibly get us out of here is if God himself picked up Grant and the entire Army of the Potomac and placed 'em down where we're headed." Joseph turned his attention back to the crack and what lay outside. "Unless he was to do that, then we ain't free and not <u>likely</u> to be anytime soon."

"No better than slaves, I reckon," Tom agreed. "Even so, it's better than Andersonville."

"Even so?" Joseph asked, turning back to Tom.

"So to speak," Tom said with a wink and a grin.

17

THURSDAY, SEPTEMBER 15, 1864

CONFEDERATE PRISONER OF WAR CAMP,
FLORENCE, SOUTH CAROLINA

Joseph walked along the center of the road with the other prisoners. There was no forming up of men or any attempt at marching, as there was at Andersonville. Here the men simply walked as if all semblance of being a soldier had been finally taken from them.

Joseph glanced behind and saw Robert and Tom close on his heels. Confederate guards lined both sides of the roadway, and Joseph noticed that most were men too old to enlist in regular units. Their appearance was shocking to Joseph. Most looked as if they hadn't eaten in some time, their uniforms hanging from their bodies as if meant for larger men.

Joseph knew from arriving prisoners at Sumter that Grant was closing in on the South and the blockade of the Southern ports had made getting food and supplies to the Southern states almost impossible, but he hadn't thought the civilians had suffered nearly as much. The look in the guards' eyes told a different story. The open hatred that radiated from their faces worried him more than the conditions at Andersonville.

Robert felt it too. "I reckon they would shoot us for a slice of cornbread," he whispered to Joseph as they walked.

They continued down the road until they reached a field surrounded by forest. Joseph saw a farmhouse and barn at the far end and a fence of wire with cans attached to make noise should anyone try to climb over. Rows of tents filled the field, but there didn't appear to be many prisoners.

The guards halted them at a flimsy gate of logs and wire, and a Confederate officer dressed in a worn uniform stepped forward to address the prisoners. Joseph saw that the man walked with a limp and used a cane.

"Welcome to the Florence Stockade, gentlemen." The officer cleared his throat. "I should inform you now that any attempts to escape will be met with deadly force. You may look at this facility and think to yourself, 'Why, this is a mere shadow of the formidable fortifications of Andersonville.' That the guards are old and feeble men, well past their prime, and that escape would be a Sunday stroll through the meadows." He pointed with his cane at the men standing guard. "I can assure you that each man here is an excellent marksman, and should you elude their eagle eyes and make it into the surrounding countryside, well, gentlemen, you are deep, deep in the South, and you have no friends outside this prison. You would be run down with hound and horse and most likely shot dead by our God-fearing citizens, and your lifeless carcass left to rot where you fell."

He limped back to stand beside the gate. "Give us no cause and you'll be treated fairly. Anyone causing riotous behavior or attempts at insurrection will be met with swift and severe punishment." He took off his hat and gave the men a brief bow. "Enjoy your stay."

"Quite the speech," Tom murmured.

"There's the Southern hospitality you were lookin' for," Joseph whispered back.

The guards led them into the field and they fanned out.

"What tent should we pick?" Robert asked.

"Over this way," Tom said.

"Where?" Joseph asked.

Tom pointed with his chin. "Over near the wire. Those tents are closest to the woods." Tom leaned in close to Joseph and Robert. "We'll need to act soon. Before they finish the stockade."

"You're a damn fool," Joseph hissed under his breath. "Look at the guards patrolling outside the wire. Barely ten feet between them."

"It's worth the chance," Robert whispered, his eyes straying to the trees.

"The chance to get us shot," Joseph said. "I'll not get myself killed because you two get an idiot idea in your heads." Joseph stopped talking as they neared the wire and the guard's attention turned to them.

Tom led them to a tent and nodded his approval. "This'll do nicely." He dropped his roll inside and sat down on the ground.

Joseph lay on his side, trying to get some sleep. The tight quarters of the tent were worsened with the addition of Tom, and Joseph tossed and turned trying to find a comfortable position. He eventually gave up and took out his diary. He wrote a couple of lines and tucked it back into his coat.

"That your diary?"

Startled, Joseph looked over and saw Tom staring at him.

"I saw you writing in it back in the railcar."

"What of it?"

"That paper is worth a lot in trade. More than the scraps of newspaper. Maybe get us some extra rations."

Joseph scowled at Tom. "It's not for trade."

"Not sayin' it is, but there are those that would do unspeakable things for that book."

"I'll keep that in mind," Joseph whispered. "Best you forgot you ever saw it."

Tom nodded. "Good night, Joseph."

Joseph rolled over and put his back to Tom. "Good night." Joseph closed his eyes and tried to get some sleep.

Joseph woke up suddenly and put a hand to the breast of his coat. He felt the diary inside and breathed a sigh of relief. He blinked his eyes and saw that the sun was up and both Tom and Robert had left the tent. He crawled outside and stood up, stretching the kinks out of his legs and back.

Looking around, Joseph realized that he missed his morning walks with Breeze and set out to stretch his legs. He wandered in and out of the rows of tents and made his way toward the farmhouse and a group of Confederate guards standing just outside the wire. He thought about approaching them to ask about rations, but the look on their faces changed his mind and he changed directions, cutting back across the field.

By noon the sun was blazing hot despite the month, and Joseph had to remind himself he was hundreds of miles south of his home. His mind drifted back and he thought about the leaves turning and the thick morning dew that covered everything. He wiped the sweat from his forehead and thought about taking his coat off but remembered the diary. He didn't want to chance it falling out and being seen.

Joseph found that an irrigation ditch had been dug cutting through the center of the field, bringing water to the camp. He knelt down and cupped his hands, filling them with water and splashing the cool liquid on his face and neck. The water revived him, and he began looking for a way back to his own tent. He wandered back to an area he recognized and found the row near the wire.

Joseph noticed two men bent near the opening of one of the tents and, as he neared, realized it was his own. He saw that Tom was asleep inside, and the men were rummaging through his haversack.

Joseph stepped up behind one of the men and kicked the man in the big muscle at the back of his leg. The man howled in pain and fell to the ground. The second man jumped to his feet and swung a length of wood at Joseph's head. Joseph ducked just in time and returned with a solid punch to the man's face.

The commotion woke Tom, and he quickly realized what was happening. He jumped to his feet just as the man with the wooden club swung a second time at Joseph.

Joseph managed to avoid the strike but got tangled up in the fallen man's legs. He looked down just as the second man swung the club again. This time the club caught the side of Joseph's head and he crumbled to the ground.

Tom "Joseph?"

Joseph moaned and opened his eyes. He saw two blurry figures kneeling over him.

Robert "Joseph! Are you okay?"

Tom "Are you still alive?" Tom asked.

Joseph "I reckon I am." Joseph put a hand to his head. "Feels like cannons are goin' off in my head."

Tom "Not surprising considering you used it to block that club."

(pain) Joseph "Help me up," Joseph groaned.

Robert and Tom lifted Joseph to a sitting position.

Joseph "What happened?"

Tom "After you got hit I had a go at 'em," Tom said proudly. "I managed to put it to them good too. They had enough and took off a-runnin'."

Joseph "Did they take anything?" Joseph asked. His hand went to his coat pocket—his diary was gone. He looked around at the ground.

Tom "Lookin' for this?" Tom asked. He held the diary out to Joseph. "One of 'em took this from you while you were out cold. I managed to get it back."

Joseph took the diary and put it back into the inside pocket of his coat. "Thank you, Tom."

Joseph, Tom, and Robert spent the next two days watching as more and more prisoners arrived. Soon the entire field was crammed with Union soldiers from various prisons.

The sound of construction reached them, and they knew that soon they would be herded like cattle into the new prison and any chance for escape would vanish.

The thought of escaping now filled Tom's waking thoughts. He paced up and down the row of tents, his eyes constantly straying to the wire and the guards just on the other side.

Joseph watched Tom for several hours before finally getting up and joining him in his pacing. "You're starting to draw attention," he warned the young man. "The guards are now watching you like a rabbit they want to cook up and eat."

Tom glanced at the guards and growled. "I tell you, Joseph, if we don't do somthin' soon, we'll be stuck here till war's end, and who knows when that will be?" He pointed at the prisoners filling the field. "They'll pack 'em in till there's no room. No water and little rations. It'll be Andersonville all over again." He grabbed Joseph's coat. "I don't mind dying, Joseph. But starvin' to death or layin' in my own vomit while the fever takes me scares me somethin' fierce."

The intensity of Tom's plea shook Joseph. He looked around at the camp and realized that Tom was right. "Unless you can come up with somethin' better than jumpin' the wire and hopin' the guards don't shoot yer fool head off, then I ain't goin'."

Tom let go of Joseph's coat and began pacing again.

"Tom, you keep this up and you'll end up in the hospital."

Tom stopped and looked at Joseph as if he had hit him between the eyes with a piece of lumber. "The hospital," he murmured. He turned and looked at the farmhouse. "Hospital," he repeated. He began walking toward the farmhouse. "I'll be back later," he called over his shoulder.

Joseph watched him go and shook his head. "He's gone completely mad."

Joseph returned to the tent and sat down. Robert returned from a trip to the latrine and sat down next to him.

"Where's Tom?" Robert asked.

Joseph shrugged. "I'm not really sure." He looked over at

the buildings, wondering what the man had in mind. He fully expected to hear gunshots. "Best get the fire going," he told Robert. "We can at least get our dinner started."

Robert managed to get a decent fire going from the scraps of wood the soldiers tossed over the wire. It was mostly warped and splintered lumber pieces from the construction of the stockade. It was dry and easily lit but burned fast.

"Hand me the rock," Robert said as he laid out the rations of salted bacon and rice.

Joseph picked up a large, flat piece of flagstone they had dug out of the ground. It was flat and thin enough to use as a skillet. He carefully placed it on the burning wood.

"I'll get water," Robert said. He picked up their tin cups and ran to the stream. He returned a short time later and rested the cups filled with water on the stone around the edges. He sat back down and waited for the water in the cups to heat up. When the water was close to boiling, he grabbed two handfuls of rice and carefully put the grains into the cups.

"Won't be long now," he said. "Soon as the water boils, I'll put the bacon on."

Joseph smiled. "You're gettin' good at cookin' with no pots or pans and little food."

"The stone's a trick my pa taught me on my first hunting trip." Robert smiled at the memory. "We shot two rabbits that time. He showed me how to skin 'em and lay 'em out on the rock once it got hot enough. I can still smell the fat sizzling." He closed his eyes. "Joseph?"

"Yeah."

"I gotta get out of here."

It was a simple statement, but Joseph could feel the intensity of what Robert was saying. "I know."

Robert began laying the strips of bacon on the stone. The sound of sizzling and the smell of the pork cooking made Joseph's mouth water. Robert busied himself fussing over the cups of rice, making sure to stir each cup so the rice wouldn't stick to the tin.

Tom returned just as the bacon and rice were ready. "Smells great!" he said, sitting down with a huge smile on his face.

"You seem better," Joseph commented. He saw that Tom's left forearm was wrapped in white linen. "What happened to your arm?"

"I cut it <u>with</u> a sharp stone."

Robert handed Tom one of the tin cups and a spoon. "You mean you cut it on a stone."

Tom set the tin on the ground and reached for one of the bacon strips. He tossed it from hand to hand until it cooled enough to stuff into his mouth. "No, I mean I cut myself with a stone."

Joseph and Robert exchanged looks. "So you're not better," Joseph said carefully.

"Oh, I'm better than better." Tom saw the looks on Joseph's and Robert's faces and laughed. "Eat your food and I'll explain."

Robert handed Joseph a tin and a couple of strips of bacon. He then sat down and waited.

"I needed to get into the hospital," Tom explained.

"Why?" Robert asked.

"Because it's outside the wire," Joseph answered before Tom could.

Tom grinned and then shoved a spoonful of rice into his mouth.

Joseph "What did you find?" Joseph asked.

Tom "The house is packed with sick soldiers," Tom answered. "Mostly dysentery. The stench is terrible." He shoveled another spoonful of rice into his mouth. "You guys should eat," he said around a mouthful of food. "The doctor goes home at night, leaving two nurses to care for the sick. There's only two guards on duty."

Joseph "That's two guards too many," Joseph grunted. "How would we sneak out of the house?"

Tom "Ah," Tom said. "There's a back door."

Robert "How did you manage to find that out?" Robert asked. He started chewing on a piece of bacon, totally focused on Tom's story.

Tom "Flies."

(Flat) *Joseph* "Flies," Joseph repeated.

Tom "Flies and mosquitoes. The house is filled with 'em. I asked the nurse that was patching me up why so many. She told me they keep the back door open to let air into the house. It helps to cool it down and keeps the smell from becoming overpowering."

Joseph "We still have the guards to worry about." Joseph said.

Tom "I agree," Tom said. "But they don't like being there 'cause of the smell and fear of catching the fever. They spend a lot of time wandering around outside. Every prisoner in there is bedridden. The thought of one of them trying to escape is the furthest thing from their minds."

Robert "So how do we get in?" Robert asked. "Cut ourselves too?"

Tom shook his head. "The guard at the wire that let me in stayed near me the whole time and then escorted me back. We need to get in and stay in and make 'em think we're really sick."

Joseph "With dysentery," Joseph commented thoughtfully. He looked at Tom. "I gotta admit, this is a better idea than jumpin' the wire and runnin'."

Tom smiled. "I thought you might like it."

Joseph "So when do we do this?"

Tom stood up and looked at the wire in front of the farmhouse. "The guards will be changing up in an hour."

Joseph "Tonight?" Joseph asked. "You want to do this tonight?"

Tom "It's only a matter of days before they have enough of the stockade finished to move us in. Once that happens, we are stuck here."

Robert "I say we do it, Joseph." Robert said. "I can't stay here much longer."

Joseph rubbed his beard in frustration. "Yeah, yeah, I know, Robert." He looked at Tom. "You're sure 'bout this?"

Tom nodded.

Joseph "Okay. We go in an hour."

Tom smiled. "Good. I'm gonna go and watch to make sure the guards change when they're supposed to. As soon as they do, I'll come back."

Robert "What you gonna do if we make it, Joseph?"

Joseph "Don't rightly know," Joseph answered. "Up till now I hadn't really thought we'd make it back before the war ended." He looked at Robert. "What you gonna do?"

Robert "If we do make it back. I reckon I'll re-up and continue fightin'."

Robert's answer took Joseph by surprise. "I thought you missed home."

Robert "I do." Robert's face took a serious look. "Mort and I talked a lot when he was still alive. He joined up because of his Negro friend and what the Southerners did."

Joseph nodded. "Henry told me."

"Mort did well in school; did you know that?"

Joseph shook his head.

"He told me that our Constitution says that every man has the God-given right to be free, and President Lincoln said the same when he declared all Negroes free." Robert took a stick and played with the fire. "I ain't never seen anyone talk with such . . ."

"Passion?" Joseph offered.

"Yeah, passion." Robert looked Joseph in the eye. "He was my friend, Joseph. Yours too. I reckon I owe it to him to keep fightin'." He smiled. "I reckon you think I'm half-crazy talkin' this way."

"No, no, I don't," Joseph said thoughtfully. "I think Henry was thinkin' the same way before he died."

"We lost a lot of people since we started. I gotta think that there's a reason for it. That somethin' good's gonna come out of it all."

Joseph smiled at Robert. "You've grown."

Tom returned, walking as fast as he dared without drawing attention. "The guards are changed," he told them. "We go now or never."

Joseph and Robert got to their feet.

Tom led them between the tents until they neared the wire. Joseph could see two guards talking.

"We gotta look sick," Tom said. "Hold your stomachs and kinda hunch over when you walk."

The three of them began walking as if they were suffering.

Robert began to shake. "I don't think I can do this, Joseph. I ain't good at fakin'."

Tom looked over at Joseph. "We gotta make it look good."

Joseph nodded. He took a couple of quick steps forward. "Sorry about this, Robert." He suddenly stopped and took a step back shoving his elbow behind him. He connected hard with Robert's stomach.

Robert doubled over and would have fallen to the ground had Tom and Joseph not grabbed him from either side. They carried Robert between them, the young man's legs dragging behind and approached the guards.

"We need to get to the hospital," Tom gasped. The strain of carrying Robert had both of them sweating.

"What's wrong?" one of the guards asked.

"Dysentery," Joseph grunted. "We all got it."

The guard tilted his head to look at Robert. "How do you know it's dysentery?"

As if on cue, Robert vomited his entire meal on the ground at the guard's feet.

The guard jumped back. "Bill," he said to the other guard.

"Yup."

"I'm gonna bring these here Yanks up to the house."

"Yup."

The guards held the wire up so the three men could pass under. He motioned with his rifle for them to continue up to the house while he walked behind, keeping a respectable distance should the one in the middle decided to throw up again.

They entered the house, and the smell of vomit, sweat, and decay in such a confined space hit them like a hammer. Everywhere they looked they saw men lying on the floor or on narrow wooden cots. A woman came hurrying up and frowned at them. "We are full up," she said, wiping her hands on an apron covered with grime.

Tom "We can't go back," Tom groaned. "Our friend here has been throwing up since morning and we're not doin' so good."

The woman ran a hand through her disheveled hair and looked around. "Bring them to the back." She led the way through the main floor of the house to a back room.

Joseph saw that the back door was indeed open and a guard sat in a chair just outside the doorway.

Woman "There." The woman pointed at a corner of the room.

Joseph and Tom dragged Robert to the corner and set him down as gently as they could. They sat down on either side of him. Joseph put his hand on Robert's forehead.

Woman "I'll bring some water," the woman said and left the room.

Joseph "How you doin'?" Joseph asked Robert.

Robert glared at Joseph.

Joseph "What do we do now?" Joseph whispered to Tom. "We're stuck in here with all these sick men."

Tom "Yeah, but we're close, Joseph. Just outside that door is the forest."

Joseph "The guards," Joseph pointed out.

Tom "Take a look around. The men here can't even lift their heads, never mind attacking a guard." Tom looked at the guard sitting in the chair. "This is where they put the worst of their soldiers 'cause it's the last place they'd think of trouble."

Joseph looked around and realized that Tom was right. He nodded. "So what do we do?"

Tom "We wait until an opportunity presents itself."

Joseph let his head slip back to rest on the wall behind him. "Wonderful," he muttered.

The sun set, and the room slipped into a dark gloom. The woman returned and lit some lanterns to give some light. Both

Robert and Tom had fallen asleep, but Joseph remained awake, his eyes watching the woman as she moved about the room, checking on the men. She appeared to be in her twenties, but working among the sick had deprived her of sleep and any opportunity to look after her appearance. Still, Joseph thought, she looked pretty.

The woman caught Joseph staring. "Don't be getting any evil thoughts in your head, Yankee man."

Joseph smiled. "Ma'am, I reckon I'm not strong enough to produce such thoughts, and even if I was, I am a gentleman." He continued to watch her. "Thank you," he said.

"You're thanking me for what?"

"For looking after us. I know you have no reason to, but you're doin' it just the same."

"I'm a Christian," she answered. She began changing the dressings on one of the men. "Sick men require care; dying men require compassion."

"Amen," Joseph said. "This your farm?"

"It was," she answered. "After my husband died I had trouble keeping things going. The army offered to pay good money to use the land."

"When did your husband die?" Joseph asked.

The woman stopped what she was doing and gave Joseph a hard look. "For a sick man you're full of questions."

"Can't sleep."

"Are you afraid you won't wake up?"

Joseph smiled. "Somethin' like that, I reckon."

The woman ran a hand through the frazzled strands of her hair. "Fear's no sin." She stood up and began folding linen bandages. "My husband was killed at Crampton's Gap."

A sudden pang of guilt gripped Joseph. He wondered if he had been the one who killed him. "I'm truly sorry for your loss." [Woman] "Loss is loss," she said. "Lost my two boys to the fever a few years back. A daughter in childbirth." She continued folding the linens as she spoke. "The Lord has his ways, and it's not for me to question." She picked up the pile of bandages. "Try to get some sleep," she said as she left the room.

Joseph watched her go, wondering how she could find the strength to go on. He closed his eyes and tried to sleep.

18

WEDNESDAY, SEPTEMBER 21, 1864

THE JOURNEY NORTH

Joseph woke to the sound of gunfire and men yelling. He looked around and saw Robert sitting up. Tom was standing near the back door. The chair the guard had been sitting in was empty. "What's going on?" he asked, getting to his feet and pulling Robert with him.

"I think someone's trying to escape," Tom answered. "We need to go now while the guards are gone."

Joseph nodded and they moved to the door.

Tom poked his head out and looked around. "It's a clear run to the trees." He crept out and then started running. Joseph and Robert followed close behind.

They got about two hundred yards from the house and

the trees were just ahead when another shot rang out. Joseph heard Robert scream from behind and he turned in time to see Robert's legs kicked out from under him.

Joseph ran back and grabbed Robert's arm. "Can you stand?"

Robert didn't answer. His eyes stared unseeing back at Joseph. The entire front of Robert's shirt was turning a dark red.

Tom ran back and grabbed Joseph by the coat. "He's dead, Joseph! Ain't nothin' we can do for him."

A low groan sounded in Joseph's throat. He let go of Robert's arm and allowed Tom to drag him away. Slowly, Joseph managed to get his legs moving faster, and soon the two were running again. Tom led the way around the edge of the swamp, keeping to drier ground as much as possible. They crashed through some underbrush and splashed knee-deep in the marsh.

"Which way?" Joseph asked.

Tom looked around and shrugged. "Not from 'round here, remember?"

Joseph growled his frustration.

The sound of hounds and men moving through the bush made the decision for them. "Come on!" Joseph barked. He pushed through the water along the bank until the water reached his chest. He pointed at some tall reeds growing out of the water. They made their way into the reeds and Joseph broke one in half. "They're hollow," he said. Joseph broke off another one and handed it to Tom.

"What do we do with these?"

"Breathe," Joseph answered. He stuck one end in his mouth and sank under the water.

Tom gaped wide-eyed at the spot where Joseph had just

been. The sound of hounds grew closer and Tom stuck the end of the reed into his mouth and dropped under the surface.

Joseph reached down and grabbed the roots of the weeds to keep from floating back to the surface. He could make out the wavy lines of the trees at the water's edge and the sudden appearance of soldiers with the hounds. The dogs padded into the water a short ways, then back to the shore a few times before moving on.

One of the soldiers pointed at the reeds, and Joseph had a moment of panic when the soldier raised his rifle and fired.

The surface of the water rippled, distorting Joseph's view, but by the time it had settled, the men were gone. Slowly he let go of the roots and rose to the surface. He felt around and grabbed Tom's arm, pulling him up. Tom surfaced and wiped the water from his eyes.

Tom "Did one of the guards shoot at us?" he asked.

Joseph "Yes, but not because he saw us. More to see what would float up if he hit something." Joseph tilted his head and listened. The sound of the hounds receded and then stopped. "Come on," Joseph said.

They climbed heavily out of the water, their clothes weighing them down. Joseph took his coat off and checked his diary. The oilcloth kept most of the water out. He gave it a quick shake as he looked at the bush around them. "We should find a place to lay up for the night."

Tom "Which way should we go?" Tom asked.

Joseph looked up and down the bank. "Downstream for now. You're probably not going to like this, but I think we should stay in the water. Just in case they come back with the hounds."

Tom looked down at his clothes and grimaced. "I reckon that's a good idea." He climbed back into the water. "You comin'? This was your idea."

Joseph put his coat back on and followed Tom downstream. They made good progress at first, but the stream slowed and the banks became muddy, and each step became a struggle. By the time they decided to leave the water, both were exhausted.

Tom crawled out and lay on his back, his chest heaving up and down. Joseph was able to remain on his feet but leaned against a tree as he fought to get his breath back.

"We need to get our clothes dry," Joseph said. He pulled his coat off and spread it over a branch. He reached into the pocket and pulled out his diary. He opened the book and hung it on a small branch to dry the pages.

He looked over and saw Tom smiling at him. "What are you grinnin' at?"

"We made it!" Tom laughed. "My plan worked!"

Joseph nodded, but he couldn't find any pleasure in escaping. Not yet.

"Why the frown? We're out! Free!"

Joseph shook his head. "Your plan came with a price. In case you've forgotten, Robert is dead." Joseph sat down on the ground and ran his fingers through his wet hair. "And we ain't free. We just moved into a bigger prison. Until we cross the lines, everyone here—soldier and civilian—is a guard."

Tom picked up a stone and tossed it in the water. "I still say we're better off than in the camp." He looked at Joseph. "Why did you agree to it? My plan, I mean."

"I agreed to it for Robert's sake. He wouldn't have lasted much longer in there." Joseph swallowed hard. "And because

I agreed, he's dead."

Tom "He died a better death than if he'd stayed," Tom argued. "Would you rather he lay sick with fever? Fightin' for his life, and all you could do is to sit beside him, prayin' that God take him quick?"

Josep "No, of course not." Joseph couldn't argue the point.

Tom "How much daylight do you think we have?" Tom asked, stripping his shirt and pants off. He found a spot where the sun filtered through the trees and laid his clothes down.

Joseph looked at the sun. "It's still morning. I reckon we got seven, maybe eight hours of good light left. More than enough to dry our clothes and figure out which way we should take."

Tom "I vote we take whatever direction gets us as far away from the South as possible."

Joseph smiled. "That would be north."

Tom "So what are your plans once we get back across the lines?" Tom asked, sitting down on the grass and letting the sun warm his body.

Joseph "Find my regiment and get back into the fight," Joseph said.

Tom "You can't be serious."

Joseph "I am," Joseph answered. "I swore an oath, Tom. Same as you. I intend on keeping that oath."

Tom shook his head in disbelief. "Why? We just been from one hell to another. You don't think that counts? I paid my debts. Sumter saw to that." Tom threw another stone into the water. "No sir. When I get back, I'm done."

Joseph "That's desertion, Tom, and you know it."

Tom "This war could go on for another ten years, Joseph. You gonna fight till then? When's it enough? When we get caught again and again and forced to live like animals over and over?"

Tom needs to get worked up in this bit.

191

Tom pounded the ground in frustration. "Just tell me why."

"Because of Robert," Joseph answered.

"Because he died?" Tom asked. "I don't understand."

"Robert realized that we was fightin' for something bigger, something more than just what the politicians wanted us to believe," Joseph said. "It's not just about freeing slaves. It's about keeping the words of the Constitution sacred. That all men are created equal." Joseph lay down on the ground. "Robert figured that out and he died for it. If his death is to have any meaning, then we carry on for him." Joseph raised up on one elbow and looked at Tom. "When we get back, you can do what you want. You can go to hell for all I care, but if you was any kind of soldier, then you'll carry on with me." Joseph lay back down and closed his eyes.

"It's still a long way back though," Tom said quietly.

"We've come this far, Tom. Get some rest."

Tom woke sometime later and saw Joseph standing on the bank, staring out at the water. "What time is it?"

"Gettin' close to sundown," Joseph answered. "We're near Florence, right? South Carolina?"

"That's what that chatty colonel at the camp said." Tom began putting his clothes back on. "We should follow this river downstream. Probably take us to the coast." He laced his boots and stood up.

"We'll head north from here." Joseph turned from the water and put his coat on. He took his diary off the tree branch and checked the pages. Satisfied that it was dry, he wrapped it up in the oilcloth and tucked it back into his coat. He looked at Tom, wondering what he should say. "So what's it to be, Tom?"

TOM "I may not have <u>known</u> Robert as long as you, but he was <u>my</u> friend too, and despite what you may think of me, I <u>was</u> a pretty good soldier."

Joseph "I believe it," Joseph said.

Tom looked at his boots. "I'll go <u>back</u> with you. I'll help you <u>honor</u> Robert's memory."

Joseph "Good enough. We should get goin'. We can put a few miles behind us before it gets too dark to see."

They started walking north, following the bank until it turned, forcing them to head into the bush. The sky clouded over and the rain started. At first it was just a light sprinkle of water, but it soon turned into a deluge. *de-li-yuge*

(shout) Tom "Kinda makes you wonder why we bothered to get dry!" Tom shouted.

(shout answer) Joseph "We should find a place to stop for the night," Joseph answered. He spotted an overhang of rock and headed in that direction.

There wasn't a lot of room, but they both managed to squeeze in enough to get out of the rain. They huddled together for the night, trying to keep warm. By morning the rain had stopped and they continued on.

At noon they came across a set of train tracks. They crouched behind a bush as a train rattled past, pulling the same type of cars they had traveled in.

Tom "Reckon that train is headed to the stockade with more prisoners," Tom said.

Joseph "Reckon so." Joseph looked up and down the tracks and crossed over. He signaled for Tom to follow.

They continued on until they reached the banks of a large river. Joseph looked at the far bank and shook his head. "Gotta be two, maybe three hundred yards across."

Tom "We can't swim it, and I don't see a boat along the bank," Tom said. "What do you want to do?"

Joseph "We keep going north. Grant was heading south with the army. I'm hopin' we meet up with them."

Tom nodded. "Makes sense. What do we do about food? I don't know about you, but my belly button is touchin' my back."

Joseph "We'll have to forage for food. Look for berries as we go," Joseph said.

Tom "Berries," Tom repeated.

Two days later they found themselves stumbling through the bush. They had traveled during the day, stopping in whatever cover they could find at night. They'd managed to find handfuls of berries, but the season was late and the birds and other animals had picked most of the bushes clean.

Joseph stopped and slumped against a moss-covered tree trunk.

Tom "Joseph?" Tom leaned on the trunk and looked down at his partner. "You okay?"

(weak) Joseph "We need to find more food," Joseph answered weakly. "We'll starve to death long before we reach our lines." He tried to stand and fell back down. He closed his eyes and fell into deep sleep.

Joseph woke to water splashing on his face. He blinked his eyes and saw Tom standing over him, holding out his hand.

Tom "Here, Joseph. Eat these." Tom held out a handful of berries.

Joseph took the berries and shoved them into his mouth.

Joseph "Thank you," he said. "We need to find food soon." He looked up at the sky. "How long was I out?"

Tom "Couple hours," Tom answered. "While you were sleeping,

I did some looking around."

"And?"

"Well . . ." Tom hesitated.

"Tell me."

"I found a cotton field. Looks like a plantation," Tom said. "I followed the edge and saw some shanties not far from here."

"Slaves?"

Tom nodded.

Joseph ran a hand through his tangled hair. "I think we should ask for help."

"From the darkies?" Tom shook his head. "They're more likely to turn us in."

Joseph pushed himself to his feet. "I don't reckon they will, Tom." He started walking. "Come on. It'll be dark soon."

Tom followed, shaking his head.

It was night by the time they reached the shanties. The buildings were a patchwork of boards and bits of lumber scrounged from the plantation.

Joseph could see a lantern in the window of the nearest building. "We'll try that one," he whispered to Tom.

"I just want you to know I'm against this," Tom whispered back. "If they turn us in and we get hung, it'll be your fault."

"I'm willin' to take that chance. Come on." Joseph led the way to the door. He raised his hand to knock, then stopped. He took a deep breath and pulled the door open and stepped inside. Tom followed close on his heels.

They found themselves facing a couple of Negro men and three women, sitting around a table. There was a stunned silence as they stared at Joseph and Tom.

Joseph saw a fire in the fireplace and a pot hanging over the flames. The smell of something simmering made his mouth water and his stomach clench.

Joseph cleared his throat. "Our pardon for the intrusion."

One of the men stood up and took a step forward. "You's from the Potter farm?" the man asked. His short, black hair was grayed at the temples.

"No," Joseph answered. "We are . . ." He searched for words to explain what they were doing there. "We're escaped prisoners of war."

"Why'd you tell 'em that?" Tom hissed under his breath.

Joseph made a shushing noise.

The older man squinted at them. "Prisoners? You escaped convicts?"

"Pa, look at what they's wearin'," the younger man said. "Them's uniforms."

The man took a step closer and gave their clothing a good looking over. "Not the same as Massuh's son is wearin'."

"That's cause they's Yankees," said the son.

"Yankees?" one of the women screamed. She stood up and grabbed a broom. "Yankee devils in our home?"

"Now, you hush, Delia. They don't look like no demon."

"How you know what a demon look like, old man? Massuh done told us they was demons, and should we ever see one, we's to tell him right off 'lessen they steal our souls!" She clutched the broom like a weapon.

Joseph and Tom stood still, stunned by what was going on around them. "I assure you, ma'am, we are not demons." Joseph tried to use as calm a voice as he could muster. "We are just lookin' for food."

The older man grabbed a length of wood leaning against

the fireplace and moved closer.

"Whatcha doin', Charlie?" the woman named Delia asked.

"I'm gonna see if they's demons." He raised the wood threat-eningly. "Now, you's just stand there peaceable-like, or I'll bash you but good."

Tom took a step back and tugged at Joseph's sleeve. "We should leave."

"Stand your ground," Joseph said.

The man moved to within inches of Joseph's face before looking behind him. "No horns or pointy ears," he said. "No tails neither." He backed up and lowered the piece of wood. "There's a wild look to you though."

"We've been walking through the bush for days," Joseph explained. "We really are starving. If you got anything to spare, we'd be real grateful."

"We ain't got no food here!" Delia shouted.

"Liar!" Tom shouted back.

"Tom!" Joseph warned. "This is their home." Joseph turned back to the older man. "If you got no food to spare, we'll leave."

Charlie looked at the others.

"We can spare a bit, Pa." One of the younger women stood up and took two bowls off a shelf.

"What if Massuh finds out?" Delia asked Charlie. "You's too old to take another whuppin'."

"We won't tell anyone," Joseph said quickly. He watched as the woman scooped out what looked like a thick stew into the bowls.

"Eat and go," Charlie said. He sat down but put the piece of wood on the table, ready to grab.

The woman approached and held out the bowls and two

spoons. "It ain't much, but it'll stick to your ribs good 'nough."

Joseph took the two bowls and handed one to Tom. "Thank you. My name is Joseph, and this is Tom."

"My name is Mary Ellen, and this is Samuel." She pointed at the young man. "And the little one over there is Martha."

Joseph gave a quick bow with his head. "Pleased to meet you." He took a spoonful of the stew and shoved it into his mouth. The taste was strange to him but welcome, and he chewed the food with a sigh.

"Best sit at the table," Samuel said. He stood up and made room for Joseph and Tom.

They ate in silence while the others watched. Joseph scraped his bowl and swallowed the last little bit. "Thank you," he said again. "That was very good."

Charlie laughed. "First time a white boy's tasted our vittles."

"Well, it was very good," Tom said with a small burp.

"Whatcha be doin' now?" Samuel asked.

"We're trying to make for the Union lines," Joseph answered.

"Where's that?"

"Don't rightly know at the moment."

"We could make for New Bern," Tom suggested.

"You know where that is?" Joseph asked.

"It's near the coast, north of here; I know that," Tom replied. "They did keep a garrison there."

Joseph nodded. "Okay, we make for New Bern."

"Well, best you start now," Charlie said. "Longer you all stays here, bigger the chance Massuh catch wind." He stood up and held on to the piece of wood. "Ain't none of us takin' a whuppin' 'cause of white boys."

Joseph and Tom exchanged glances.

Joseph "You're right, of course," Joseph said. "We've put these good people in danger long enough." He rose to his feet and motioned for Tom to do the same.

Samuel got to his feet. "It won't do you to be tryin' to leave tonight. Most like, youse'll end up gettin' caught." He looked at Charlie. "They can sleep in the lean-to out back."

Charlie scowled.

Sam "No good givin' me that look, Pa. You knows it same as me. Besides, theys'll get caught shor 'nough if Massuh come here."

Char "I'll not be whipped."

Sam "I'll take the whippin', Pa." Samuel waved for Joseph and Tom to follow him outside. He led them around the back of the shack. "It ain't much, but it'll keep the rain off, and you can pile some of that wood and hide behind it."

Joseph "Thank you," Joseph said. He waited for Samuel to leave, but the man remained where he was. "You can stay and talk if you want."

Samuel nodded.

Joseph looked around for something to sit on but ended up settling down on the ground. Tom sat beside him, and Joseph motioned for Samuel to sit.

Samuel hesitated for a moment, then sat down and crossed his legs. "You really escape from the stockade at Florence?"

Joseph "Yes," Joseph nodded.

Sam "Ain't never talked with a soldier. We's not allowed to talk to white folk unless to answer a question."

Tom "Do you have any questions for us?" Tom asked.

Samuel looked around as if the mere act of talking to a white person would get him whipped. "We hears they's niggers like us fightin' up north. Wearin' same as you got on."

Joseph "It's true," Joseph said. "The Fifty-fourth Massachusetts. I saw them march past once. As proud and courageous a group of men as I've ever seen."

Samuel just stared, wide-eyed.

Tom "Samuel, do you know how we can get to New Bern?" Tom asked.

Samuel scratched the side of his face. "Never heard of such a place," he said thoughtfully. "Massuh sometimes takes me to Wilmington with him when he's doin' his business. It's north of here and near 'nough to the coast."

Joseph "How can we get there?" Joseph asked.

Sam "Well, if'n it were me, I'd follow the Pee Dee to the Little Pee Dee."

Joseph "What's the Pee Dee?"

Sam "Them's rivers. I could take you there next eve. You'd have to keep hid tomorrow." He looked over his shoulder at the shack. "I'd best talk to Pa. He's a good man, but he's had his share of whippins in his time. He's just a-scared is all."

Samuel rose to leave.

Joseph "We do thank you for everything,' Joseph said.

Samuel gave a quick nod. "I's come by in the morning before I start."

Joseph and Tom watched Samuel leave before making an area to lie down. The nights had cooled with the autumn season, but the lean-to and piles of wood offered protection from any cold breezes. Both men rolled over exhausted but with their bellies full.

Joseph woke to Samuel shaking him gently. He sat up and smiled at the man. "Mornin'." Joseph gave Tom a shove with

Joseph

his foot and was rewarded with a groan.

"Mornin' it is," Samuel said. "Best you two get inside before Tobias comes 'round."

"Tobias?"

"He's lead hand," Samuel answered. "As cruel a nigger as you'll ever meet." Samuel waved them to hurry.

Joseph and Tom followed Samuel into the cabin.

"Mary Ellen kept some bread and freshly churned butter on the table, and they's fresh water in the bucket." Samuel opened the door and looked out. "Best you stays inside till I come back."

Joseph and Tom spent the day looking out the window or talking about different routes they might take and what they might encounter.

The sun was hovering above the western horizon when Samuel finally returned with Charlie. Both were dirty and sweating heavily from their work in the fields.

Charlie scowled at them as he entered the cabin. "Well, did you's have a good day, massuhs? Sittin' in the shade all nice and cool?"

Joseph's face reddened at the jibe. "We stayed inside," he said.

"Well we's had a good day too. No whuppins, and a day with no whuppins is a good day." Charlie grabbed a piece of bread off the table. "Needs to wash up." He left the cabin, slamming the door behind him.

"Don't go mindin' my pa. He barks like a hound at most folks, 'cept the massuh." Samuel looked out the window. "Sun be down soon. We'll leave then."

Charlie returned and sat down at the table. "I expects you white boys be wantin' some vittles to take wit' you." He cackled. "Well, what we got in the cupboard? Looky there," he said, pointing to an empty shelf. "Vittles fit for a king." He laughed again.

"Pa, you knows they ain't gonna be food till Mary Ellen finishes up dinner at the main house," Samuel said. "She gets to bring back any leftovers," he told Joseph and Tom. "We'll be long gone 'fore she's done."

"That's fine," Joseph said.

They waited until the sun set before Samuel led them out and around the back of the cabin. He cut a straight line across the plantation, heading north until they reached the banks of the Pee Dee River. Samuel held up his hand and moved to a large bush near the water's edge. A short time later he waved, and Joseph and Tom helped Samuel pull a small, flat-bottomed skiff out of the underbrush.

Joseph and Tom carried the boat to the water, Samuel bringing up the rear with a pair of paddles. They set the boat down on the bank.

"This be the Pee Dee," Samuel said. "Follow it downstream till you see the Little Pee Dee. You's gonna have to paddle upstream from there."

"Thank you for all your help, Samuel," Joseph said. He held out his hand.

Samuel looked at the hand and then at Joseph but didn't move to take it.

"When a man holds out his hand," Tom explained, "it's customary for the other man to shake it." He held his hand out too.

"Ain't never shook no white man's hand 'fore."

"Ain't never shook no Negro's hand before," Joseph said with a grin.

Samuel's face broke out in a smile, and he laughed. He took Joseph's then Tom's hand in turn. "If'n you two ain't the strangest white folk I ever done meet." He turned with a wave and disappeared into the night.

Joseph and Tom pushed the skiff into the water and let the current pull them along. They decided it would be best not to row until morning to make sure they didn't miss the Little Pee Dee.

Morning found them floating near the middle of the river, and they paddled the boat to the far side and began keeping an eye. They spotted the smaller river just after noon, and they paddled in earnest to put as many miles behind them as they could. By late afternoon they had to drive the skiff onto the bank to avoid paddling past farmlands that bordered the river.

They dragged the boat into the bushes and hid it as best they could.

"It's a good thing we got nothin' to eat," Tom complained. "I don't think I could raise my arms to put the food in my mouth." He sat down heavily against a tree.

Joseph groaned as he tried to stretch life back into his arms. "We gotta keep goin'." He hauled Tom up and they pushed on.

Once the sun set, their pace through the forest slowed considerably. Several times they were forced to go out of their way to avoid crossing open fields and farmsteads. By midnight they were exhausted and bleeding from scratches caused by crawling through scrub and undergrowth to avoid people.

Tom stopped and sat on the ground. "I can't go another step, Joseph. It's been at least two miles since we last saw anyone."

"We should keep going," Joseph said, kneeling down next to Tom. "Besides, there's no place to hole up for the day. We'd be caught right quick out here."

"What's that?" Tom asked pointing.

Joseph looked where Tom was pointing and saw the dark outline of a building.

Tom got to his feet and moved closer. "It's a barn," he whispered.

"We can't sleep in a barn," Joseph warned. "We'll be caught for sure."

"We can sleep in the loft. I want somethin' softer than a bed of ground and hard rocks." He moved into the open, crouching as he went.

Joseph followed on Tom's heels. "I don't like this," he whispered.

"We'll be gone before anyone knows we been there." Tom moved to the door and opened it slowly. He disappeared inside, leaving Joseph outside.

Gritting his teeth, Joseph followed. It was almost pitch-black inside, and they had to feel their way around. "We'll never find the ladder to the loft," Joseph whispered.

"There's hay in this corner," Tom whispered back. "Come on."

Joseph followed and found Tom already lying in the hay. Despite his misgivings, the hay looked comfortable, and Joseph was too exhausted to argue. He lay down next to Tom and fell into a deep sleep.

"Gentlemen."

Joseph woke with a start and opened his eyes to see an elderly lady, well dressed, holding a rather large, strange-looking pistol at his head. His eyes moved from the woman to a young black man holding a pitchfork on Tom.

"Gentlemen," the woman repeated.

Joseph elbowed Tom in the ribs before slowly rising to stand with his hands in the air. Tom rose and stood next to Joseph and put his hands up.

"That's much better." The woman smiled. "Now, before we start the formalities, I should like to discuss the pistol in my hand."

"It's a very nice pistol, ma'am," Joseph said.

"It belonged to my late husband. I sent him to Atlanta to purchase a couple of slaves, and the old fool returned with this." She dabbed a lace handkerchief under her nose to ward off the barn odor. "It's called a LeMat. Do not inquire as to why it is called that, because I do not know. What I do know is how to discharge its contents, and I believe at this distance even an old woman such as myself would not miss."

"I believe you." Joseph tried to smile warmly. "I promise that neither I nor my friend here will do anything to warrant you pulling that trigger."

"Very well, then," the woman continued. "I'm guessing from your dress and your manner of speech that you two are Yankees. Soldiers in the Union Army, if I'm not mistaken."

"Not at all, ma'am," Tom began. "We come from Kansas on our way to Charleston to buy a slave."

The woman pointed the pistol at Tom's head. "You must think me addlepated, sir. You have neither the speech of someone from Kansas nor the wherewithal to purchase a slave." She eyed both of them up and down. "You're half-starved without a penny to your name."

"You're right, of course," Joseph said. "It was wrong of us to lie."

"Well then, let us try telling the truth before I shoot you as simple trespassers." She took a couple of steps back and gave them another appraising look. "Union soldiers," she said as if talking to herself. "And from all appearances, I'd say escaped prisoners."

Joseph and Tom stood silent, watching the pistol swing back and forth, flinching ~~some~~ each time it was trained on them.

Ellen "Your silence confirms my observations," the woman said. "Well," she continued, dropping the pistol to her side, "no sense continuing this conversation here. Follow me to the house, gentlemen." She abruptly turned on her heels and strode out of the barn with surprising vigor.

The black man with the pitchfork motioned for Joseph and Tom to follow.

"The man behind you is one of my slaves. His name is Jim Young, and should you harbor any ill will towards my person, he will assuredly perforate your hide."

Joseph and Tom followed the woman, with Jim following close behind.

Joseph "Yes, ma'am," Joseph said. "Might I inquire as to your intentions regarding us?"

Ellen "My intention is to feed you," the woman answered. "And I think a bath and change of clothes will be in order as well. Both of you stink."

Joseph "Yes, ma'am."

She led them into a huge, whitewashed house. Once inside, the woman stopped and turned to face them.

Ellen "Now that we know each other's intentions, I believe introductions are in order." She smiled warmly at them. "My name is Ellen MacIntosh; however, propriety dictates that you refer to me as Mrs. MacIntosh."

Joseph gave his head a brief bow. "A pleasure, Mrs. MacIntosh. I am Joseph Hoover, and my companion is Thomas Ryan."

Mrs. MacIntosh gave a quick curtsy. She produced a small silver bell from a pocket and gave it a single ring. A young black woman appeared from another room. "Martha, see to baths for these young gentlemen."

The woman gave a curtsy. "Yes, Mrs. MacIntosh." She hurried away, calling out names as she went.

"There now. Once you two are smelling reasonably less like barn animals, we shall have to see to your clothing." She rolled her eyes to the ceiling as she thought. "I believe Mr. MacIntosh was of similar size and shape."

Martha returned with two other slaves carrying buckets of steaming water.

Ellen "If you gentlemen will follow Martha upstairs, she will prepare your baths. I have matters to attend to. Dinner will be at eight this evening." She gave them a quick head bow. "Until then, good day." Mrs. MacIntosh turned and left the house.

Martha led the two men into a side room on the second floor. Two wooden bathtubs sat in the middle of the floor and had been filled with hot water, and a small table with soap and scrub brushes had been placed between the tubs.

Martha "They's towels there," Martha pointed out before leaving the room and closing the door behind her.

Tom almost tore off his clothes and gingerly lowered his body into the steaming water, a sigh escaping his lips. He looked over at Joseph, who stared at the tub with a worried look on his face.

Tom "You just gonna stand there?" Tom asked. "It's a hot bath.

When was the last time you had a hot bath?"

Joseph "The night before I enlisted," Joseph answered quietly. He looked around the room and shook his head. "I don't feel safe here," he said.

Tom "Well, you can stand there and stink and worry about it, or you can sit in hot water, get clean, and worry about it."

Joseph "I reckon you're right." Joseph stripped off his clothes. He took out his diary and placed it on a sideboard before slipping into the water. He ducked his head under the water and came up spitting. "That does feel better," he said.

He grabbed the soap and began washing.

Martha returned with an armload of folded clothes.

Both Joseph and Tom sank lower into the water as the woman placed the clothes on a sideboard. "Mrs. MacIntosh says you be wanting to change into these clean clothes."

Joseph "Thank you," Joseph said. He waited for Martha to leave before continuing to wash.

"Ah," Tom sighed, leaning his head back. "This does feel grand."

Joseph "Don't get used to it," Joseph said.

Tom "You worry too much," Tom chided. "The old lady is harmless, and we're finally gettin' some of that Southern hospitality."

Joseph "Could be you're right, but I won't stop worrying until we get back to our own lines."

Tom "Suit yerself," Tom said, scrubbing his feet.

They sorted through the clothes after their bath and managed to find pants and shirts that fit reasonably well. They found jackets hanging in the wardrobe, and by the time they left the room, they resembled little the fugitives that had fallen asleep in the barn.

The house slaves provided a good lunch, which they wolfed down before spending the day wandering about the house. Joseph found nothing to indicate they were in danger and slowly began to relax. He strolled into the barn and found the slave Jim Young mucking out the stalls.

"Afternoon, sir," Jim said, pausing for a moment. "Is there anythin' I can do for yerself?"

Joseph smiled and shook his head. "No, Jim. I was just walking around."

"Time sorta slows down here, don' it?"

"I reckon it does." Joseph picked up a pitchfork and began mucking out one of the stalls.

"Whatcha doin', sir?" Jim asked, alarmed.

"I used to muck out the stalls on my farm up north," Joseph answered. "This reminds me of home."

"If'n Mrs. MacIntosh sees you, I'll be in deep trouble," Jim said. "You best put that fork down so's you don't get Mr. MacIntosh's things all dirty."

Joseph leaned the pitchfork against the stall door. "Sorry. I don't want to get you in trouble." Joseph found a stool and sat down. "Have you been here all your life?"

"No, sir. I was born on another plantation. My ma, she still there." He paused and thought for a moment. "Leastwhiles I think she is." Jim continued cleaning the stalls. "I was sold to Mrs. MacIntosh and been here ever since."

Joseph looked at Jim as he worked. The thought of being taken away from his family, never to see them again, was something he'd never considered. It was something that he knew would tear him apart, and yet Jim talked about it as being part of his life. "Do you miss your ma?"

Jim "Yessuh." He kept working with his back to Joseph. "I prays for her every night. She must be an old woman now." He stopped working. "I wonder if'n she's still alive."

Josep "They wouldn't tell you if she died?"

Jim "Don't reckon so. Why would they?" Jim moved to another stall. "I should finish my chores."

Joseph got to his feet. "I'm sorry about your ma," he said. "I don't reckon I could stand for that."

Jim turned around and looked at Joseph. "That's 'cause you be a freeman. Slaves like me got no choice." He turned away and headed into another stall.

Joseph left the barn and walked slowly back to the house. He looked around at the property as he went and saw several slaves working around the buildings, and a dozen more toiling in the fields. Joseph wondered how many of them had been sold away from their families.

He found Tom sitting in the kitchen, eating a cold chicken leg. "Where you been?" Tom asked.

"Just wandering around." Joseph sat down.

Tom "Still worryin'?"

Josep "I reckon so. I just got this feelin', is all," Joseph said. "I'll be happier as soon as we're on our way again."

By evening Joseph's anxiety had increased, and he found it almost impossible to sit still. He paced about the great room like a caged animal. Tom sat near the fire, watching with an amused look on his face.

Martha entered the room and informed them that dinner was being served. She led them into the formal dining room, where they found Mrs. MacIntosh waiting with two young women.

Ellen "Well, I must say, you two gentlemen clean up quite nicely." She smiled. "I'd like to introduce you to my daughters, Elise and Morgan MacIntosh. Ladies, I present Mr. Joseph Hoover and Mr. Thomas Ryan. They are escaped Yankee soldiers."

Elise and Morgan curtsied with a slight giggle.

Joseph and Tom bowed awkwardly.

Ellen "Elise and Morgan only recently returned from my sister's plantation outside of Atlanta." Mrs. MacIntosh waved her hand at the table. "Shall we sit?" As if on cue, two well-dressed black men came forward and held the chairs for the ladies.

Joseph and Tom took their seats once the women had sat down.

More slaves emerged from the kitchen area with bowls of soup.

Ellen "I've had the cook prepare a goose for tonight's dinner, in honor of our guests." Mrs. MacIntosh began slurping her soup.

Joseph and Tom took several sips of the soup. "It's very *Joseph* good," Joseph commented.

Mrs. MacIntosh smiled. "I daresay even warmed water with some pepper would seem a feast compared to what you're accustomed to."

Joseph smiled.

Silence enveloped the table save for the sounds of eating. Once the soup had been eaten, the slaves returned, taking away the empty bowls. They came back shortly with a large plate filled with slices of goose meat.

Joseph's mouth began to water at the smell of the cooked meat. The slaves dished out the meats, potatoes, and green vegetables, as well as gravy.

Ellen "As cut off as we are," Mrs. MacIntosh began, "we are always thirsting for stories about the outside world." She paused, waiting for a response. "Perhaps you can enlighten us with tales of the prisons?"

Joseph looked up from his plate and wiped his mouth with the linen napkin. "I would hesitate to bring such images to this fine table," he said. "I reckon it's enough to say men live in horrible conditions and starve daily."

Ellen "Yes," Mrs. MacIntosh agreed, looking at her daughters. "I believe that would be a discussion for another time. It would be more prudent to choose another topic. For instance, the purpose of this war, which, I must confess, eludes my perceptions."

Joseph looked unsure of what to say.

Ellen "It is my understanding that your Mr. Lincoln wishes to free the slaves." She made a disapproving clucking noise. "I have no objections to you Northerners living without the slaves," she said. "What I object to—and I believe this is a common thread throughout the South—is the very idea that we in the South should follow this incredulous line of thought."

Joseph cleared his throat as he tried to think of something to say in answer. He realized that a misspoken word could create problems.

Tom "We are fighting to bring the South back into the Union," Tom interjected before Joseph could answer.

Daughter "But we are quite satisfied living our lives outside the constricts of Northern rule," the daughter named ~~Ellen~~ *Elise* said. "I for one would be lost without the attentions of our slaves."

Tom "You do realize that, should the Union win this war, that is exactly what you would be made to do?" Tom said as he shoveled in more of the goose.

Elise ~~Ellen~~ shook her head. "Impossible," she declared. "We have infinite faith in General Lee's abilities to send the Yankee hoard fleeing back to their cold and colorless lives."

Ellen "Why, I do believe, dear, you have made a pun." Mrs. MacIntosh smiled.

The girls giggled into their napkins.

Joseph smiled uncomfortably. "Very clever of you," he said.

The meal ended, and Mrs. MacIntosh's daughters excused themselves.

Ellen "We have reached the point in the evening when the men would retire to the library for cigars and brandy. As you can see, you are the only men present, so it falls to me as your host to join you." Mrs. MacIntosh rose from the table and beckoned for them to follow.

She led them into a richly appointed room with shelves of books lining the walls. A roaring fire burned in the fireplace, and several comfortable, high-back chairs sat around the hearth. She sat in one of the chairs and motioned for Joseph and Tom to sit.

Another well-dressed slave brought glasses of brandy and produced a wooden box of cigars. Both Joseph and Tom accepted the cigars, nodding their thanks to the man who served them.

Joseph took a drag of his cigar and began coughing. Tom laughed as he puffed on his own.

"I take it you are unused to cigars, Mr. Hoover." Mrs. MacIntosh smiled.

cough *smoke Joseph* "This is the first cigar I've ever smoked," Joseph conceded.

Tom "I, on the other hand," Tom put in, "have smoked many; however, none so fine as this." He took another puff and sipped the brandy with a sigh.

Mrs. MacIntosh nodded approvingly.

213

"Mrs. MacIntosh," Joseph began. "I don't wish to be rude, but what are your intentions regarding me and Tom?"

"Why, merely to help out a pair of travelers," she answered. "I also offer you the comforts of my home for as long as you wish to remain. I would find it comforting to have men about the place again."

"It's a tempting offer, ma'am," Tom said, finishing his brandy. "A man could get used to this lifestyle."

"Well, I'll leave you the night to decide. Tomorrow morning you can either stay or be on your way." Mrs. MacIntosh rose from her chair.

Both Joseph and Tom rose as well.

"I will bid you good night." She rang the small bell she kept on her person. "Martha will show you to the rooms I've had prepared." Mrs. MacIntosh left the room.

"I like her," Tom said. He went to the table where the brandy was kept and poured himself another glass.

Joseph looked around at the books and the opulent furnishings. "I reckon a spider's web would look as attractive to a fly."

Tom downed his drink. "Well, maybe it won't feel as sinister in the morning."

Martha entered the room and stood waiting. She led them up the stairs and down the hallway to doors at the end. She opened the doors and left.

Joseph entered the room and saw that a bed had been prepared. His old clothes had been washed and mended, and he placed his diary on top of the folded clothes. He lay back in the bed and put his arms behind his head, thinking about his talk with Jim and Mrs. MacIntosh. He thought about how much both their lives would change should the Union win the war.

He doubted that Mrs. MacIntosh would be able to afford her plantation if she suddenly had to pay her workers.

He also worried about tomorrow. He couldn't shake the feeling that they were in danger despite the kind offer the old woman had presented. He closed his eyes and tried to force the thought from his mind.

Joseph woke to the soft shaking of hands and a whispered voice. "Wake up, Mr. Joseph."

Joseph opened his eyes and saw the faint outline of Jim standing over him. The sight startled Joseph, and he opened his mouth to shout.

Jim clamped a hand over his mouth. "Please, Mr. Joseph. You and Mr. Tom are in terrible danger," he whispered, checking the door nervously. He slowly took his hand away.

"What are you talkin' about?"

"Mrs. MacIntosh, sir. She's done sent for the Owenses, next county over."

"I don't understand."

Jim pulled Joseph until he was sitting on the edge of the bed. He began handing Joseph his clothes. "You's is escaped Yankees. Mrs. MacIntosh and the Owenses capture escaped soldiers for the reward money."

"I thought things looked too good."

"Yessuh. The Owenses had caught a Yankee three days ago and transported him to the courthouse in the next county. Otherwise you'd be in chains by now."

Joseph finished dressing and tucked his diary under his shirt. He grabbed for his uniform coat but realized it would make it impossible to blend in should they need to leave the forest.

"We need to wake Tom," Joseph whispered. He went to

215

the door and opened it slowly, then moved to the room where Tom lay sleeping and entered. He moved quickly to the side of Tom's bed and placed his hand on his mouth before shaking him awake.

Tom's eyes flew open wide.

"Tom, it's me, Joseph." He pulled his hand away and put a finger to his lips. "We need to leave now."

"Why?" Tom hissed under his breath.

"Jim came to warn us. Mrs. MacIntosh plans to turn us in for a reward."

Tom looked from Joseph to Jim and back to Joseph. "Are you sure?"

"I don't think Jim would risk a beating if it wasn't true." Joseph grabbed Tom's arm. "Get dressed. We don't have much time."

Tom got dressed in his old clothes. He gave the new clothes one last look before nodding to Joseph that he was ready.

Jim led the way out of the room and down the stairs. "We can go out through the kitchen," he whispered.

As they passed through the main entrance, every little creak of the floorboards sent a bolt of panic down Joseph's back.

They entered the kitchen. The fire in the big fireplace had burned down to coals, and Jim silently urged them forward. He opened the back door and slid outside. Joseph and Tom followed close behind. The light on the eastern horizon marked the coming morning.

"The sun'll be rising soon enough," Jim said. "Mrs. MacIntosh mustn't find me with you. I'll take you to the edge of the plantation, but that's as far as I go." He led them past the barn and then froze.

Joseph and Tom followed his gaze and saw three men on horseback approaching.

Jim "They's here," Jim said. "Oh, Lord, they's here."

Joseph "Run!" Joseph yelled. He turned and began running as fast as he could toward the tree line. He could hear Tom close behind. Joseph slowed and risked a look over his shoulder. Jim hadn't moved. "Jim! Run!"

Context "Hold right there, nigger!" one of the men yelled. He held a whip in his right hand.

Jim saw the whip and ran.

Joseph ran as fast as he could. He caught up with Tom at the trees and turned to wait for Jim. The black man reached the forest, and the three continued on as fast as they could.

The men on horseback reached the trees and dismounted, following on foot.

Joseph could hear the others crashing through the same underbrush. A shot rang out, spurring them on even faster. Joseph jumped over a large tree root and landed in a small hollow. He pulled Tom and Jim down, and they all hid behind the huge root. Joseph saw that Jim's right arm was bleeding. He nodded at the wound.

Jim saw the blood but shook his head.

They heard footsteps coming close. Joseph moved to the trunk of the tree and pressed up against it. A young man rounded the tree and saw Tom and Jim hiding behind the root.

Joseph leapt on the man as he raised a hatchet above his head. He wrenched the handle out of the man's grasp and flung him to the ground. He pounced and held the blade next to the man's throat. "Make a sound and I'll cut your throat."

The young man went limp.

Jim "That's the young Owens," Jim said. "His name is William."

William "My pa is gonna whip you raw, Jim," William grated.

Joseph pushed the blade into the man's neck. "Where are the others?"

William clenched his jaw shut.

"Maybe I'll chop off an ear," Joseph warned. "Tell me where they are."

William groaned. "They gave up the chase. Went back to the horses."

Joseph looked around. "Tom, double back to make sure he's tellin' the truth."

Tom nodded and moved off quietly through the trees. He returned a couple of minutes later. "He ain't lying, Joseph. There's no sign of 'em followin'."

Joseph grabbed William by the front of his shirt and lifted him off the ground. He swung the young man around and slammed him against the tree. "I suggest you not follow us if you value your life."

"Joseph, we can't let him live. He'll bring the others down on us." Tom grabbed the man. "He was going to turn us in!"

"I'll not kill an unarmed man, let alone one that's hardly out of boyhood." Joseph let William go. He flipped the hatchet around and struck the man on the side of the head. William collapsed onto the leaves, unconscious. "That will give us some time."

He looked over at Jim, who was sitting on the ground, rocking back and forth. "Can you keep going?"

Jim looked at his arm. "It but grazed me," he said. "I guess I gots no choice but to go on."

Joseph "Which way?"

Jim "Which way you wants to go?" Jim asked.

Joseph "North. We need to get back to Union lines."

Jim pointed in the direction they wanted to go.

Tom "You sure?" Tom asked. He looked at the sky. "The clouds hide the sun."

Jim "Don't need no sun." Jim walked over to a tall, straight tree. "Mr. MacIntosh used to take me wif 'im when he was huntin'." He pointed at some moss growing high up in the tree. "He says moss grow mostly on the north side o' trees."

Joseph smiled. "My pa used to tell me the same thing."

Jim led the way, and they made good time as the growth beneath the trees thinned out, but by noon they were exhausted.

Joseph called a halt under a big pine tree, and they took cover under its low-hanging branches. Joseph crawled over to Jim. "Let me take a look at that," he said, pointing to the man's arm.

Jim "Yessuh."

Joseph examined the wound. "The ball just grazed you," he said. "You're lucky. If it had hit straight on, you'd have lost the arm." Joseph used the knife to cut a piece of his shirttail off and tied it around Jim's arm. "This will stop the bleedin'."

Tom "So what do we do now?" Tom asked. "We got no food and we're following moss."

Joseph "Jim, do you know where New Bern is?" Joseph asked.

Jim shook his head. "Don't know no New Bern. What's there?"

Tom "The Union army," Tom answered. "And freedom."

Jim "Don't mean much to ol' Jim," the black man said, shaking his head. He crossed his arms and hid his face. "I is contraband now. They catch me and they's gonna whip me. Mayhaps they'll hobble me for runnin'."

Joseph sat down next to Jim. "Why did you help us?"

Jim lifted his head. "I saw the man they caught before. When they took him away. Saw an almighty fear in his eyes." He looked at Joseph with fear in his own eyes. "Mrs. MacIntosh owns me, but I couldn't let them take you away. Not anymore."

"You thought you could warn us without Mrs. MacIntosh findin' out," Joseph said quietly. "That was a brave thing you did for us."

"Don't know about brave," Jim said. "Now I's contraband. They catch me too far from the plantation, they'll just hang me. I seen 'em do it. Left him hangin' for all to see as a warnin'."

"We'll just have to make sure they don't catch us." Joseph patted Jim on the shoulder. "Come on. We should keep moving."

The trio continued moving north for the rest of the day, Jim checking the trees to make sure they were still heading in the right direction. They reached a river shortly before the light began to fade, and Joseph suggested they find a place to bed down for the night.

They found a hollow under an overhanging rock and filled it with dead leaves for bedding. Joseph checked Jim's bandage. "It doesn't look infected," he said.

Tom sat down in the leaves with a groan.

"What's wrong with you?" Joseph asked.

"I should have eaten more at the old lady's house. I'm starving."

"We could try fishing," Joseph suggested.

"With what? No line or hook." Tom looked around. "I reckon we could use a tree branch for a rod."

Joseph smiled. "We don't need that." He left the hollow and

went to the riverbank. He found a spot where the current slowed and swirled gently around an outcropping of rock. Joseph pulled up his sleeves and lay down on the rock. He carefully put his hands into the water up to his elbows, his face almost touching the surface.

Tom and Jim watched with fascination as Joseph remained prone on the rock for several minutes.

"What's Mr. Joseph doin'?" Jim asked.

Tom shook his head.

Joseph suddenly plunged his arms deeper into the water. "Ha!" he yelled before tossing a large trout onto the shore.

Tom grabbed the fish before it could flap itself back into the water and held it up. "Well, I'll be a son of a donkey."

Joseph returned to his vigil, his eyes scanning the shallow water, waiting for another fish to swim into the calm area. A few minutes later he drove his arms into the water again and pulled out another fish. He threw it to Jim and stood up, shaking the water from his arms.

"Well, I never," Jim said, holding the fish up.

"Neat trick," Tom said with a grin. "Now all we need to do is get a fire going."

Jim began collecting dead branches. He made a small pile of leaves and stacked the branches over them. Then he pulled a piece of flint from his pocket and used the hatchet blade to get a small fire going.

They cleaned the fish and hung them over the flames to cook. When they were done, the three men wolfed down the meal and then lay down in the leaves.

The baying of hounds in the distance woke them. Joseph smothered the remains of the fire and moved to the edge of the hollow. He peered into the dark but couldn't make out anything but the nearest trees.

The hounds barked again.

Jim began to shake. "Hounds," he panted. "We'll be caught for sure." He tried to run from the cover of the overhang, but Joseph tackled him and pinned him to the ground.

"If you run, they'll surely hear you," he whispered.

Jim struggled. "They's comin'!"

Tom piled onto Jim and helped hold him down. "Quiet, for God's sake. You'll bring 'em right to us!"

"Jim," Joseph whispered. "we won't let them take you. I promise."

The sound of the dogs reached them again, and Joseph cocked his head. "They're on the other side of the river," he breathed. "Probably chasing an animal."

Jim slowly relaxed, and Joseph rolled off him. "As soon as it's light enough to see, we'll get moving."

Tom patted Jim on the shoulder and rolled over to try and get some sleep.

The three men continued on for several more days. Each time they neared the river, Joseph would manage to catch enough fish to keep them from going hungry. The rain continued on and off, but the sky finally cleared and the sun appeared.

They found the river again and Jim stopped. He looked around as if remembering something.

"What is it?" Joseph asked.

Jim pointed at the riverbank and they saw a half-submerged dock. Jim went to the bank and pulled on a rope he found tied to the dock. A boat floated into view and he stepped back.

"Jim, what is it?"

"I knows this place," he said. Jim looked around and found a path leading away from the river. "I was born near here."

"Do you remember how to get there from here?" Joseph asked.

Jim pointed down the path. "This will take us to the plantation where my ma had me." He moved slowly down the path.

"Maybe we shouldn't, Joseph," Tom said, looking around nervously. "The last time we went on a plantation, we ended up getting shot at."

"It be okay," Jim said. "We can get help from the slaves." He took a few more steps.

"You want to see if your ma is still alive?" Joseph asked quietly.

"Yessuh."

"We'll go with you." Joseph turned to Tom. "I know *I* couldn't go on without finding out."

Tom threw up his hands. "I'll be holdin' you responsible if we get shot at again."

They followed Jim along the path until it reached a small clearing and a run-down cabin. Jim slowed as he neared, as if afraid. "What if she is dead?" he whispered.

Joseph put a hand on Jim's shoulder. "Only way to find out," he said.

Jim nodded and took another step toward the cabin.

The door opened, and a small, gray-haired woman limped out, carrying a bucket. She stopped when she saw Jim. "And what be you needin'?" she asked.

Jim stood with his mouth open, but no words came out.

"Speak up, boy." She moved closer and squinted her eyes.

"Oh my sweet Lord. It can't be. Jim? Is that you?"

Tears began flowing down Jim's cheeks. "Yes, Mama. It's your Jim."

The old woman dropped the bucket and limped forward.

Jim fell to his knees as his mother reached him, and they embraced.

"Jim, oh my Jim," she wept. "I never thought to see you again."

"It's okay, Mama."

Joseph and Tom stood back, feeling awkward.

"How?"

Jim pulled out of his mother's arms and got to his feet. "I came with them."

The woman looked at Joseph and Tom. "They's your new owners?"

"No, Mama." Jim hesitated.

"We're Union soldiers," Joseph said. "My name is Joseph Hoover, and this is Tom Ryan."

"This is my ma, Dora."

"I don't rightly understand, Jim. Whatchoo doin' wit' Yankee soldiers?"

"Your son helped us escape," Joseph said.

Dora's eyes went wide. "Oh, Jim. You's a runaway?"

Jim bowed his head.

"Jim, oh my Jim. They's gonna catch you and hang you."

"He's comin' north with us," Tom interjected. "We don't plan on gettin' caught."

"You gotta get outta here, Jim. Simon is the overseer now. He's gone right mean. He'll turn youse all in and whup you till you bleed."

"Dora!" a distant voice called.

"Oh Lord, Jim, he's comin'." She looked at Joseph and Tom. "Get in the cabin and keep quiet, now. I'll try to get them on their way." She pushed them into the cabin. "Now, hush," she said, closing the door.

"Dora! Where you at, old woman?"

Two men strode around the corner of the cabin. One of the men was black and carried a bullwhip curled at his hip. He towered over the white man, who carried an old musket over his shoulder.

"Massuh Daniels," Dora said with a curtsy. "Simon."

"Didn't you hear me callin' you?" Simon asked.

"I's an old woman, Simon. Don't know which is worse, my ears or my eyes."

Daniels held up four partridges hanging from strings. "Here," he said. "Be quick and clean these."

Dora took the birds but didn't move.

"I'll be wanting those now," Daniels said. He propped his musket against the cabin and started for the door.

"Wait!" Dora cried out. "It's hot in the cabin, Massuh Daniels. You'd be more comfortable sittin' out here while I clean these here birds."

Daniels eyed the old woman. "What's in the cabin, Dora?"

"Nothin'. Ain't nothin' in there, massuh."

"Simon, go in and see what she's hiding."

Simon strode to the door and put his hand to the latch. Before he could touch it, Joseph opened the door and stepped through. Tom and Jim followed.

"Well, well," Daniels said. "What have we here?"

"They's just a couple of white men with their slave. They wanted water."

Daniels turned on Dora and backhanded her hard. She fell to the ground. "You're lyin', old woman."

Jim lunged forward. "Mama!"

Daniels ran to his musket and trained it on Joseph and the others. "Who are you?"

"It's just like the old woman said," Joseph explained, putting his hands in the air. "We are just passin' through. It was hot, and we saw the cabin."

Daniels looked hard at Jim. "This here's yer slave?"

Joseph nodded. "We bought him a few weeks ago."

"Massuh," Simon said, looking at Jim, "I knows this nigger." Simon looked at Dora, then back at Jim. "Well, if it ain't Jim Young." Simon sneered at Jim. "And all growed up."

"Jim Young," Daniels repeated. "I sold you to the MacIntoshes years ago."

Dora crawled over to Daniels and put a hand on the man's leg. "Please, Massuh Daniels. Don't be hurtin' my Jim."

"You done run away," Simon said. He untied the whip and let it snake out on the ground. "I'll tear the hide off'n you, boy."

"No!" Dora screamed.

Daniels raised his musket and drove the butt into the side of Dora's head. She collapsed to the ground and lay still.

"Mama!" Jim ran to his mother, lifting her head into his arms, and rocked back and forth. "Mama?" He lifted his head, tears rolling down his face. "She's dead." He looked at Daniels with pure hatred. "You done kilt her."

Daniels looked at Dora and then at Jim. "She was old," he said. "Wasn't worth the food to keep her." He looked back at Joseph and Tom. "So, couple of white boys helpin' a runaway. We hangs the likes of you." He waved the musket. "Simon, go and get some rope."

Jim let out a growl and charged at Daniels. Daniels managed to bring the butt of the musket around and catch Jim in the stomach. Jim dropped to his knees.

Daniels raised the musket to bring the butt down on Jim's head but Joseph lunged past Simon and grabbed the musket before he could strike.

Simon turned and raised the whip but Tom jumped on the big man from behind and tried to wrestle the whip away from him.

The musket fired as Joseph and Daniels struggled for control, and the kick from the discharge caused Daniels to lose his grip. Joseph flung the musket away and slammed his fist into the other man's face. Daniels's nose exploded, blood spraying onto his face.

Joseph threw him to the ground and grabbed Simon. Tom was still clinging to the big man's back as Joseph repeatedly hit Simon about the face and head. Simon finally fell to his knees.

"Come on!" Joseph yelled. He grabbed Jim's shirt and yanked him to his feet. They ran as fast as they could back down the path toward the river. When they reached the bank, Joseph untied the rope while Tom helped Jim into the boat. Joseph shoved off and they floated away and downriver just as Simon reached the shore. He stopped in his tracks and watched them float away.

"Why you stoppin', boy?" Daniels screamed as he reached the bank. He carried his musket and began loading it.

"I can't swim," Simon said.

"Bout as much use as the old woman!" Daniels finished loading the musket and aimed. He pulled the trigger.

Joseph heard the shot and felt the bullet pass through the loose fabric of his shirt just under the arm. He jerked to the side and the boat overturned, dumping everyone into the river. The side of the boat struck Joseph's head, and he sank beneath the water.

Tom "Joseph!" Tom called out.

Jim took a deep breath and dove under. It seemed to take forever, but he finally broke the surface of the water several feet from the overturned boat, with Joseph tucked under one arm. He managed to swim to the boat, dragging Joseph with him, and they clung to the sides as the boat continued to drift downstream.

Daniels managed to reload and fire off one more round that struck the keel of the boat before they were swept around a bend and out of sight.

Tom let the boat float downstream for some time before finally paddling to shore. Tom and Jim let go of the boat, and they dragged Joseph up the bank.

Tom "Joseph?" Tom shook his friend until Joseph's eyes fluttered open. "Good. You're not drowned." Tom lay back and caught his breath.

Jim "You okay, Mr. Joseph?" Jim hovered over him.

Joseph "I'm fine, Jim." Joseph raised up on his elbows. "Are you okay?" he asked the black man.

Jim sat back and shook his head. "He done kilt my Ma."

Joseph "I know, Jim. I'm sorry."

Jim "It's 'cause of me he done kilt her. If'n I hadn't showed up, she'd still be alive."

Joseph "No, Jim. I reckon that man was full enough with hate that he'd have found any reason to do what he did." Joseph pushed himself to a sitting position. "I'm glad you got to see your ma again."

Jim "Thank you, Mr. Joseph," Jim said.

Joseph "Thank *you* for saving my life. I'd have surely drowned if you hadn't grabbed me." Joseph looked over at Tom. "How are you doing?"

Tom "I'm fine considering we got shot at again," Tom said pointedly.

Joseph "Yeah. Sorry about that," Joseph said. He looked at the sky. "It's almost night. We should move into the forest more. Just in case they try following the river for a while."

Jim and Tom helped Joseph to his feet, and they made their way through the trees. They traveled as long as the light held, but soon they could not see enough to keep from tripping over the smallest of roots and stones. They found another pine tree and crawled under the branches.

They had just settled in when a strange sound reached their ears.

Tom "You hear that?" Tom asked.

Joseph "Sounds like singing," Joseph said. "I don't think I've ever heard singing like that before."

Jim "I has," Jim said. He crawled out from the low-hanging bows. "It's Negro singing."

Tom and Joseph followed Jim out from under the tree.

Joseph "What kind of singing?"

Jim smiled at the memory. "After work on Sunday we all gather about the fire and sing praises to the Lord." He started walking toward the singing.

Tom "Whoa, Jim." Tom held up his hands "We just got away from one crazy master with a musket. I don't intend to get close to another."

Jim "Won't be any white folk there," Jim said. He moved around Tom and continued walking. "'Cept the two of you."

Joseph "Come on," Joseph said, waving his hand. "Third time's the charm."

Tom "I can't believe I'm doing this," Tom moaned, following behind.

Jim led them into a clearing with a huge fire. At least twenty slaves were gathered around the fire, all singing and keeping time by clapping their hands. As soon as they saw Jim, the singing stopped, and they all turned to look at the newcomers.

An older black man with gray hair stood up and raised his *Emerson* hand in greeting. "Welcome," he said. The old man started forward but stopped when he saw Joseph and Tom emerge into the firelight.

Jim "They's friends," Jim said quickly.

Joseph held up his hands to show they were unarmed.

Emerson "It's a strange night when a nigger calls a couple of white boys friends." The old man took a few more steps from the group. "Your names, sirs?"

Joseph "I'm Joseph Hoover, and this here is Thomas Ryan."

The old man nodded and turned to Jim. "I may not know your name, but I know a runner when I sees one. My name is Emerson."

Jim "Jim."

Emerson "Well, Jim, you are welcome at the fire, and if they truly be your friends, then I reckon they can join as well."

Joseph "We don't intend to interrupt your singing," Joseph said. "We can sit on the ground here and just listen."

Emerson smiled. "You're very kind, but we'll not have guests sitting on the ground." He waved them toward the fire.

"Make room."

Space was made, and Joseph, Jim, and Tom sat down.

Emerson remained standing as he spoke to the faces turned to him. "We all gathered here as equals in the light of the fire. We all gathered here as sinners and we all gathered here lookin' for a reason. Lookin' for comfort and healin' and looking for salvation."

"Amen," several slaves affirmed.

Emerson looked at Joseph and Tom as he continued.

"We all livin' in strife. We all live in suffering, but through our strife, through our suffering, we come to know the face of our Lord, and in acceptin' our sins in this life, we find ourselves on the banks of the river Jordan and that one more river to cross."

There were more amens, and then a young woman stood and raised her voice in the song "River Jordan." Her voice echoed around the clearing so strong and clean that Joseph found himself standing with the others, clapping his hands in time.

When the song was over, he sat back down. The slaves began to leave in ones and twos until only Emerson was left. He turned a keen eye to Joseph. "You seemed to like that song," he said, his face breaking into a warm smile.

"I ain't never heard anything so beautiful," Joseph said.

"The music comes from the heart and soul, and so it touches the heart and soul of them that listen."

Two women returned to the fire, carrying bowls and blankets. Emerson handed Joseph and his companions the blankets, and the woman placed the bowls in their hands.

"You are wet, cold, and hungry," Emerson said. "We can

talk while you eat." He looked at Jim, who had barely looked up from the fire.

"He saw his mother beaten to death earlier today," Joseph explained. "I ain't never seen such brutality, and I've been in the war for almost two years."

"It is somethin' we live with every day." Emerson placed a comforting hand on Jim's knee. "Your ma, what was her name?"

"Dora Young," Jim answered.

"I thought as much. The Daniels plantation is the closest one, and I done many an errand there." Emerson shook his head. "I knew your ma. She was a good woman. You should rest easy, Jim Young, in the knowin' that she rests in the arms of our Lord and watches down on you even now."

Jim nodded but kept silent.

"Those at the Daniels plantation are unusually cruel," Emerson continued. "One would think the devil hisself bred those boys."

"Well, they have no love for us," Joseph said. "I'm sure I broke his nose."

"Violence begets violence."

"Amen," Tom said.

Everyone looked at him.

Tom shrugged. "I went to church," he said defensively. "Once."

"I'll take a guess that you boys be headin' north," Emerson said.

"Yes," Joseph answered around a mouthful of stew.

"New Bern?" Emerson asked.

"Yes," Joseph said, a bit surprised.

"We help a lot of runaway slaves get to the Union garrison

there." He smiled. "We can help you."

Tom "Freedom," Tom sighed. "There were times I never thought we'd make it. Me and Joseph escaped the prison camp at Florence, and we've been runnin' ever since."

Emerson "We's all slaves to somethin' or someone in this life. The real freedom comes after, and until then it's what we do in this life that leads us to freedom or slaves to eternal damnation."

Joseph "'For they have sown the wind, and they shall reap the whirlwind,'" Joseph said, remembering his Bible verses.

Emerson "Amen," Emerson said.

Joseph "How far till we get to New Bern?"

Emerson rubbed his chin. "Possible two, mayhaps three more weeks. One of us will guide you to the next point in the road you'll be takin'. We only know that far in case we get caught. From there someone else will take you the next leg."

Joseph "Makes sense," Joseph said. "When can we leave?"

Emerson "Tonight," Emerson said. "Once there, you'll have to wait one, maybe two days before someone shows. Best have Jim here meet them first. Seeing two white boys will send 'em runnin' for sure."

Joseph looked at Tom, who nodded. "Jim?" Joseph called. "Do you want to come with us?"

Jim looked at Emerson for an answer.

Emerson "We can hide you for a while if'n you choose to stay. But the Danielses will be by at some point, and they'll want to search the property."

Jim "I reckon I started out with Mr. Joseph and Mr. Tom. I feel responsible to them. I'll make sure they get back."

Emerson "What will you do if you make it back to your Union lines?" Emerson asked.

Joseph "We'll rejoin our units and keep fightin'." Joseph said.

Emerson "Why?"

The question caught Joseph off guard.

Tom "To protect the Constitution and preserve the Union," Tom said proudly. "And to free the slaves," he added.

Emerson nodded. "That's what they tells you at the start, and it's a fine enough reason."

Joseph "It's not enough," Joseph said quietly.

Emerson gave Joseph a knowing look.

Joseph "I've lost more friends—my brothers, really—than I care to count. I've seen the suffering of men on both sides, and until I was captured, I never fully understood what slavery meant." Joseph looked at Jim grieving for his mother. "How a man can be torn away from his home and family at the whim of someone else. Bought and sold with no more thought than sellin' a horse." Joseph took a deep breath and let it out. "I gotta believe that somethin' better is gonna come out of this. That's what I'm fightin' for now. Somethin' better."

Jim "Amen," Jim said.

Emerson "Amen," Emerson repeated. "As soon as you boys finish your stew, one of our guides will take you to the next meetin' spot."

They finished their meal and a young black boy arrived. He was barefoot and his clothes looked more like rags stitched together, but he smiled at the men and waved for them to follow.

The boy led them through the forest in total darkness. Several times Joseph wanted to ask the boy if he knew where he was going but he kept silent, and soon they emerged from the trees to a smooth trail. They followed the trail for several more hours until the boy stopped suddenly. He pointed to a group of boulders huddled together just off the path. "You be waitin' there till night. Tell whoever comes 'River Jordan.'"

Before they could thank the boy, he smiled, waved, and ran back down the path the way they had come.

Tom "What do we do now?" Tom asked.

Josep "I guess we hide in them boulders and wait," Joseph said, heading toward the formation.

The next night a young woman arrived, and after a brief conversation with Jim, she led them throughout the night to the next point.

They spent the next several nights repeating the same thing over and over. Sometimes the person would bring food, and each time the guide would give Jim a word or a Bible phrase to say to the next person leading them. During the day they would sleep as best they could, and each night would find them being led like the blind through the countryside.

Joseph kept track of the days in his diary. They arrived at a fence bordering a field just before sunup on the morning of October 18. The guide pointed to a large tree before leaving them on their own.

They made their way to the tree and found the remains of a stone wall. They sat down with their backs to the cold stone, exhausted from the night's journey.

Tom "Think we'll have to wait more than the day?" Tom asked.

Twice during the trip they'd had to spend two days waiting for their guide to show. The second day was always hard wondering if the guide would show or if the Rebs had found the route the slaves were taking in their run for freedom.

Joseph "I reckon we just got to wait and see," Joseph answered. "Best get some rest though. Jim says the last guide told him this would be the last leg. After this we are on our own."

Tom tucked his arms in and rolled onto his side. He was sleeping almost as soon as his head touched the ground.

Joseph kept watch on the path and the far tree line. Jim sat next to him, staring at the ground at his feet. "You haven't said more than three words these last few days," Joseph said.

"Been thinkin', is all."

"'Bout what?"

"What's gonna come of me once we cross the line," Jim answered. "Got no family to stay with. No one to take me in."

Joseph hadn't thought about that. "Did you do any smith work for Mrs. MacIntosh?"

"I can make and shoe a horse," Jim answered. "Repair wheels off'n the wagons good 'nough."

"When we get back, we'll see about gettin' you a job with a livery stable in New Bern. If not there, some other place."

Jim looked at Joseph. "You'd do that fer me?"

"You saved our lives, Jim. Mine twice. I'd have surely drowned if you hadn't dove after me."

Jim smiled, then got to his feet. "I can hear a stream just down this hill. I need some water."

"Don't take too long," Joseph said. "We should stay together."

Jim disappeared around the tree, and Joseph laid his head against the stone and closed his eyes.

He woke to a clicking sound that he knew all too well. He opened his eyes and stared down the barrel of a bayonet-tipped musket. At the other end was a Confederate soldier. A second click brought his head around and he saw another soldier holding his rifle on Tom.

"You boys looked like you was havin' a nice nap," said the

first soldier. "Might we ask what're you doin' near a nigger meetin' hole?"

"Meetin' hole?" Joseph repeated. He shook his head. "Don't know nothin' 'bout no meetin' hole."

"We was just takin' a rest after a long walk," Tom said. He caught movement out of the corner of his eye and saw Jim crawling in the grass toward them.

"Where was you walkin' from?"

"Florence, South Carolina."

"That's a far ways to walk," the soldier said.

"'That's why we was restin'." Tom smiled.

Jim rose up out of the grass directly behind the second soldier and grabbed the hatchet that hung on his hip. Before the soldier could react, Jim struck him hard across the back of his head. The soldier folded into the ground.

Jim pounced on the other soldier and grabbed the rifle from behind. He brought the rifle up and pulled it tight against the man's throat, throttling him.

Joseph and Tom sprang to their feet and kicked the soldier's feet out from under him, and they all fell to the ground. A shot rang out, and Tom clutched his left arm, yelling as he fell.

Joseph looked down the hill and saw a mounted Confederate soldier cocking his pistol for another shot. Joseph grabbed the pistol from the soldier Jim was choking and fired first. The mounted soldier slumped in the saddle before falling off. Spooked, the horse took off at a gallop.

Jim finally let go of the soldier he was holding, and Joseph trained the pistol on him.

"Tom, are you okay?" Joseph asked. He risked a quick look at his friend.

Tom rolled to a sitting position and held his right hand over the wound in his arm. "Well, I been shot."

"Jim, we need something to tie this man up with." Joseph nodded at the soldier lying on the ground. "Is he dead?"

Jim went over and rolled the man onto his back. Wide-open eyes stared back at him. "He's dead," Jim said. "I done kilt him."

"You had no choice, Jim." Joseph motioned for the other soldier to kneel. "Jim, I need you to tear that man's shirt into strips and tie this one's hands behind his back."

Joseph kept the pistol pointed at the man's head as Jim did as Joseph said. When Joseph was sure the man was secure, he went to Tom and reached for his arm. "Let me take a look at that." He examined the wound. "You're a lucky man, Tom Ryan. Had that been a mini ball instead of a pistol round, you'd be missing an arm right now."

"Feels like it's gonna come off anyhow," Tom groaned.

Joseph grabbed one of the strips from the dead soldier's shirt and bound the wound. "Bullet went clean through." He tied the strip in a knot. "Can you use the arm?"

Tom grimaced, but he was able to move the arm up and down. "Seems okay," he said.

Joseph picked up the pistol and turned on the other soldier. "What unit are you with?"

"I ain't tellin you nothin'."

Joseph punched the man in the face and then pointed the pistol at his forehead and cocked the hammer. "Only gonna ask one more time."

"Sixth Battalion, North Carolina Cavalry."

"Cavalry," Joseph muttered. "Where are the other horses?"

"Back at camp. We got word that escaped niggers was meeting

here on their way north. We were sent here to watch the area."

"That's not good, Joseph," Tom said. "The others that come will be caught."

Joseph frowned. "We'll have to leave a message of some sort so they'll know not to come here anymore."

"I'll stay," Jim said.

"You can't stay, Jim," Joseph said. "You're contraband too. They catch you, they'll hang you."

"I knows it." Jim looked Joseph in the eye. "I got nothin' waitin' for me where you is goin'. We both knows that. I'll stay here until the guide comes and I'll head back."

"You sure you wanna do that?" Tom asked.

"I think it's what I'm supposed to do." He stood up and dragged the soldier over to the tree and began tying him to the trunk. "I'll bury the other soldiers."

Joseph nodded, then headed down the hill to the other dead soldier. He heaved the body onto his shoulder and carried it back to the tree. "We'll take their uniform coats and kepis."

He stripped both of the bodies and helped Tom into one of the coats. When they were done, they looked like Confederate soldiers. Joseph took the holster and strapped it to his waist.

Tom picked up one of the rifles and began loading it. His injured arm hampered him a bit, but he soon had it loaded and slung over his shoulder.

Joseph loaded the other rifle but kept it in his hand. He rested the butt on the ground and took one more look at Jim. "Last chance, Jim."

Jim shook his head.

Joseph held out his hand. "It's been an honor, Jim. I wish

you all the luck and Godspeed." Jim took the hand, unsure of the offer.

Tom stuck out his hand. "We would not have made it this far if it weren't for you, Jim."

Joseph and Tom started walking north again. They continued on, despite it being daylight, trusting to their new uniforms.

By night they had made several miles and decided to leave the path they were on and head into the bush. They had only traveled a short way when Joseph spotted a fire up ahead. He silently warned Tom and crept forward. Through the trees he spotted several Confederate soldiers seated around a campfire, laughing and making their supper.

They returned to the path and continued on for several hours before they felt safe enough to bed down for the night. They lit no fire. The only food the soldiers back at the tree had carried were pieces of cornbread. They tasted stale, but Joseph and Tom ate them anyway.

"Back at Sumter we would have considered this a feast," Joseph commented, chewing on the crumbly bread.

"Those are memories I would sooner leave behind," Tom said.

For the next several days, they traveled north using old trails and fields to avoid any contact with Confederate soldiers. By the morning of the twenty-fourth, they found themselves lying in deep grass, watching Confederate soldiers digging trenches on a picket line.

"What do you think?" Joseph asked.

"I think we're on the wrong side of that line, wearing the wrong uniforms," Tom whispered back. "But since we are wearing the wrong uniforms, why don't we just try walking our way past?"

Joseph shook his head. "As soon as we get close enough, we'll be challenged, and they'll know or at least suspect we're not what we appear."

Tom "Well, we have to do something soon. I'm starving, and we have no idea where we are. New Bern could still be weeks away." Tom raised his head and looked to their left. "Why don't we try and go around the picket?"

Joseph pursed his lips, trying to think of a better idea, but he eventually agreed.

They backed away and began walking west.

Jeph "Best get your rifle at the ready," Joseph suggested. "At least then we'll look like we're a patrol."

Tom unslung his rifle.

They walked a couple of miles before turning north again. They stopped when they came upon the far side of the field.

Tom "Is that a Union line on the other side of the field?" Tom asked.

Joseph squinted. "It is!"

Conf "Hush, you two!"

The voice took them by surprise, and they looked around.

Conf "Up here!"

Joseph and Tom looked up and saw a Confederate sniper in the trees. "You idiots are makin' enough noise to tell those Yankees exactly where I am."

Joseph "Sorry," Joseph whispered up.

Conf "What are you doin' this far out?"

Tom "Patrol," Tom answered.

Conf "What unit you with?"

Tom "Seventh Battalion, North Carolina Cavalry," Tom answered.

Joseph's eyes flew wide as he realized Tom's mistake.

Cont "Seventh? Ain't no Seventh anymore!"

Joseph looked up and saw the sniper trying to bring his rifle to bear. He drew the pistol at his hip and fired. The sniper slipped off the branch, but his ammunition pouch caught, and he ended up hanging upside down. There were several cries of alarm from the Confederate line, and several soldiers began running toward them.

Tom "That's done it!" Tom yelled. "Run, Joseph!"

Both men took off running across the field toward the Union line. Rifles began firing, and they could hear mini balls hitting the ground all around them. They reached the halfway point when smoke appeared from the Union line and more bullets began singing past their ears.

Joseph "They're both shootin' at us!" Joseph yelled.

Tom found an old crater from a previous battle and dove headfirst into it. "Joseph! Over here!"

Joseph reached the lip of the crater and tumbled into the bottom. Tom was already wrestling with his ammunition pouch, trying to get it off so he could take the Confederate coat off.

Tom "Get your coat off, Joseph, before both sides kill us!"

Joseph managed to get his coat off and crawl to the northern edge of the crater. He saw a couple of Union soldiers taking aim and ducked back down just as the bullets tore chunks of grass where his head had been. He popped his head back up while they were reloading. "Hey!" he yelled. "We're Yankees!"

The soldiers paused for a second. One of them called down the line, and an officer came running over.

Officer "Who are you?" he called out.

"Sergeant Joseph Hoover of the 121st Volunteer Infantry out of New York!" Joseph yelled back.

There was another pause. "What does your unit call themselves?"

Joseph smiled. "Onesers!"

"Then get yourselves over here! And hurry!"

Joseph grabbed Tom, and they crawled out of the hole and into the tall grass. The Confederates began firing again, and the officer ordered covering fire. By the time they reached the Union lines, both Joseph and Tom were filthy and covered with scrapes. Two soldiers dropped their rifles and hauled them over the berm and into the trench.

Joseph and Tom lay there, breathing hard, before finally looking at each other and breaking into hysterical laughter.

19

TUESDAY, OCTOBER 25, 1864

NEW BERN, NORTH CAROLINA

Joseph stood outside the quartermaster's building, adjusting his new uniform. The sergeant's stripes on his arms glowed a bright white in the morning sun.

The door behind him opened, and Tom stepped out and into the bright sunlight. "How do I look?" he asked.

Joseph gave him a mock critical look.

Tom unslung his rifle and held it at the ready.

Joseph "Well, considering everything is new, I'd have to say you look ready."

Tom smiled and slung his rifle back over his shoulder. *Tom* "What about you, Joseph? You ready?"

Joseph nodded. "I reckon it's time long overdue to get back into it."

"My boat leaves at high tide later today," Tom said. "You?"

"I'm here for a few more days, then a long train ride back to my unit."

"At least you won't be packed into a cattle car."

"There is that." Joseph laughed.

They stopped as a company of soldiers marched past.

Joseph grew somber at the sight of the young men heading to their next battle.

"You still think too much," Tom commented.

"Just remembering," Joseph said. "Remembering a lot of faces. Ash, Mort, and Jacob. Henry and Jerome."

"Robert," Tom added.

"Yes," Joseph sighed. "Robert."

"I admire you, Joseph."

"You do? Why?"

"Even though they were only in your life for a short time, they were your friends. You've found your reason for continuing the fight. For something better, but you can fight for them too." Tom stood at attention and held a salute. "To the Union, the Constitution, and to something better."

Joseph smiled and returned the salute. "And to friends."

Tom held out his hand. "You take care of yourself, Joseph Hoover of New York."

Joseph took the hand warmly. "You too, Thomas Ryan of Maine."

Tom winked and spun on his heels and marched down the street.

Joseph watched him go, then turned and headed back to his tent.

AFTERWORD

Joseph Hoover rejoined his unit at Winchester, Virginia, on December 1, 1864. He fought in the Appomattox Campaign and was injured at Petersburg on April 2, 1865, where he managed to capture the Confederate soldier who shot him.

Joseph was sent to City Point Hospital and later transferred to Carver Hospital in Washington, DC, where he witnessed the funeral procession of President Lincoln from his hospital window.

Joseph was discharged from the Army along with the rest of his regiment on May 30, 1865, having completed his full three-year term of service to his country.

After the war, Joseph married Mary Dygert, and their descendants keep alive the memory and spirit of Sergeant Joseph Hoover of the 121st New York Volunteer Infantry to this day.

ABOUT THE AUTHORS

Michael Davis is a native of Sao Paulo, Brazil, and founder and CEO of Uptone Pictures. Davis has been developing television shows, nationally syndicated radio shows, docudramas, and direct-to-home movies for twenty years. He consistently strives to put "imagination in motion," to produce quality content that motivates, inspires, and entertains audiences. He has a BA in communication arts and literature from Cedarville University. He lives in Raleigh, North Carolina, with his wife, Wendi, and his two kids, William and Isabella.

William R. Walters is a retired police officer and forensic investigator and a Civil War enthusiast. Walters consults on forensic matters including police and forensic procedures on TV and movie sets. A lover of horses, Walters lives in the country with his wife, Wilma.

HE WENT TO WAR TO FREE SLAVES,
BUT WAS FREED BY THEM.

UNION ★ BOUND
BASED ON A TRUE STORY

MOVING BOX ENTERTAINMENT UPTONE PICTURES & WEATHERVANE PRESENT A MICHAEL DAVIS PRODUCTION DIRECTED BY HARVEY LOWRY

SEAN STONE RANDY WAYNE TANK JONES ISAAC C. SINGLETON JR. RUSTY MARTIN CHRISTIAN FORTUNE TRISH COOK DAVE BLAMY

EDITED BY JOHN ERRINGTON CINEMATOGRAPHY BY JOHN ERRINGTON CO-PRODUCER KARA WILLIAMSON EXECUTIVE PRODUCER BYRON JONES "UNION BOUND" BASED ON THE DIARY OF SRGT. JOSEPH E. HOOVER

ART BY JACK EAGEN PRODUCED BY KARA WILLIAMSON WRITTEN BY ALEX BOYD FIRST ASSISTANT DUANE JOURNEY MUSIC BY CRAIG BRANDWYNNE

MUSIC THEME BY DANE BRYANT-FRAZIER ORIGINAL CONTENT BY CACTUS MOSER VFX BREAKIRON ANIMATION

MOVING BOX ENTERTAINMENT   uptone PICTURES   WEATHERVANE

Directed by Harvey Lowry and produced by Michael Davis, *Union Bound* is an amazing
true story of honor, integrity, love of country, and the belief that all men are equal.

Thank you for choosing to read

UNION ★ BOUND

If you enjoyed this book, we hope that you will tell your friends and family. There are many ways to spread the word:

Share your thoughts on Facebook or your blog or Tweet "You should read #UnionBound by Michael Davis and William R. Walters // @worldnetdaily

Consider using the book in a book group or small group setting.

LIKE the book on Facebook at facebook.com/Unionbound

Write a review online at Amazon.com or BN.com

Subscribe to WND at www.wnd.com

Visit the WND Superstore at superstore.wnd.com

WND Books

A WND COMPANY • WASHINGTON DC • WNDBOOKS.COM

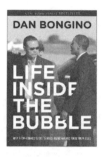
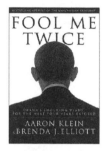

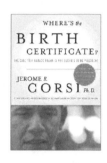

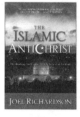

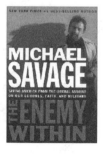
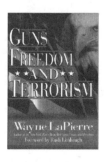
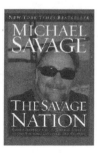

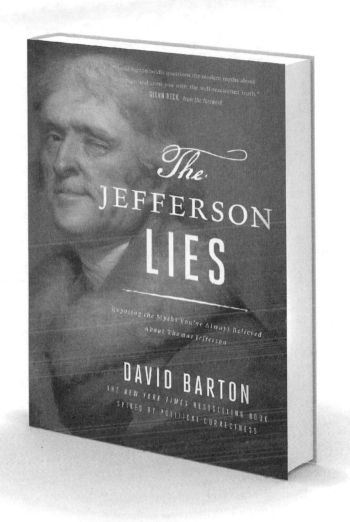

"David Barton boldly questions the modern myths about Jefferson and arms you with the well-researched truth."
GLENN BECK *from the foreword*

The JEFFERSON LIES

Exposing the Myths You've Always Believed About Thomas Jefferson

DAVID BARTON

THE NEW YORK TIMES BESTSELLING BOOK
SPIKED BY POLITICAL CORRECTNESS

This new paperback edition of THE JEFFERSON LIES re-documents Barton's research and conclusions as sound and his premises true. Through Jefferson's own words and the eyewitness testimony of contemporaries, Barton repaints a portrait of the man from Monticello as a visionary, an innovator, a man who revered Jesus, a classical Renaissance man, and a man whose pioneering stand for liberty and God-given inalienable rights fostered a better world for this nation and its posterity. For America, the time to remember these truths is now.

WND Books • WASHINGTON DC • WNDBOOKS.COM